CENTENARY ESSAYS ON DANTE

CENTENARY ESSAYS
ON DANTE

by members of the
OXFORD DANTE SOCIETY

Oxford. University. Dante Society

CLARENDON PRESS · OXFORD
1965

Oxford University Press, Amen House, London E.C.4

GLASGOW NEW YORK TORONTO MELBOURNE WELLINGTON
BOMBAY CALCUTTA MADRAS KARACHI LAHORE DACCA
CAPE TOWN SALISBURY NAIROBI IBADAN ACCRA
KUALA LUMPUR HONG KONG

© *Oxford Dante Society 1965*

Printed in Great Britain by
The Camelot Press Ltd., London and Southampton

Contents

Preface

FOR 1921, the sixth centenary of Dante's death, Paget
Toynbee had privately printed for the Oxford Dante
Society *A Record of Forty-four Years* (Clarendon Press,
1920). That record is here, in an Appendix, repeated and
brought up to date, for the seventh centenary of Dante's birth,
another forty-four years later, with, however, only a bare list of
members and without the detail of meetings, papers and dis-
cussions that Toynbee compiled with his usual precision. But
a note on the foundation of the Society by Dr. Edward Moore
in 1876, and on its purposes and habits, is added.

Toynbee at the same time compiled for the British
Academy *Britain's Tribute to Dante in Literature and Art:
A Chronological Record of 540 years* (Oxford University
Press, 1921) and accompanied it with *Dante in English Art:
A Chronological Record* (*c.* 1745-1919,) his *Dante Studies* and
his celebrated edition of Dante's letters: *Dantis Alagherii
Epistolae* (Clarendon Press, 1920). We hope shortly to see the
Epistolae reprinted, since nothing has come near to super-
seding it. The promised volume in Michele Barbi's series
shows no sign of following the *Convivio* and *de Vulgari
Eloquentia*. Toynbee's *Dante Dictionary* (in full *A Dictionary
of Proper Names and Notable Matters in the Works of Dante*,
Clarendon Press, 1898) will in this septcentenary year be
reissued in Oxford, as revised by the American scholar,
Professor Charles S. Singleton.

In these days of Epigoni, only a much more modest
tribute than the work of one member for 1921 is here
offered, a mixed bag of studies by some members of the
Society, to show that Dante still 'fa lo Scotto e l'Inghilese',
not, we hope, 'folle' but devoted, and that 'dopo se fa le
persone', if not 'dotte', at least lit by his lantern and eager
to follow 'dietro a le poste de le care piante'.

Death has already claimed our oldest contributor (aged
eighty-five, when he wrote on 'Dante and Bridges') and
oldest member (1911), Professor Cesare Foligno.

C. H.

Dante's Use in the *Divina Commedia* of the Medieval Allegories on Ovid

C. A. ROBSON

I

I N the complex art of the *Divina Commedia*[1] critics have generally admitted the co-existence of 'real' and 'imaginary' figures; but it would be an impossible task to draw the line sharply between them. At the one end of the scale we have Dante's own contemporaries and recent historical personages; at the other, purely legendary and fictional characters. It could be argued that characters actually encountered by Dante on his journey and situated by him in some determinate place in the other world, are real; those who are merely referred to for the sake of a literary allusion may well be imaginary. Some, however, belong to both classes: Jason's expedition to Colchis is cited as a mythological parallel in the *Paradiso*—but Jason himself suffers in the *Inferno* for his desertion of Hypsipyle and Medea. The protagonists of Roman history seem solid enough; but 'the taskmaster of Purgatory', the 'Cato-figure' whom Dante never names, is an ideal creation who combines features of Virgil's lawgiver ('his dantem jura Catonem')

---

[1] The principal works cited below are: Edward Moore, *Studies in Dante. First Series: Scripture and Classical Authors in Dante* (Oxford, 1896); Giovanni di Garlandia, *Integumenta Ovidii*, ed. Fausto Ghisalberti (Milan, 1933); F. Ghisalberti, 'Arnolfo d'Orléans: Un cultore di Ovidio nel secolo XII', *Mem. del R. Ist. Lombardo di scienze e lettere* xxiv (1932), 157–234 (text of the prose *Allegoriæ super Ovidii Metamorphosin*, pp. 201–29); F. Ghisalberti, 'Giovanni del Virgilio espositore delle "Metamorfosi",' *Giornale Dantesco* xxxiv (1933), 1–110 (text of the *Allegoriæ Librorum Ovidii Metamorphoseos*, pp. 43–107). References in roman numerals to the books of the *Metamorphoses* are in capitals, to the cantos of the *Commedia* in small letters.

I wish to thank Dr. R. W. Hunt and Professor C. Grayson, to both of whom these Ovidian researches owe much for advice and encouragement at a critical stage.

with the heroic resister and martyr for liberty's sake, Cato of Utica, who was Dante's favourite hero in antiquity. On the other hand Ulysses, who according to one critic 'could hardly have been more than a fiction' to Dante,[1] may have acquired a spurious reality for medievals from the Trojan histories of Dictys and Dares. There is obviously a wide zone of uncertain allegiance lying between the territories of the imagined and the real.

There were of course limitations in theory to this poetic fusion of the really existent and the conceptual. Pagan mythology was explained by medieval Christians in one of two ways: either the gods and demi-gods were evil spirits unjustly divinized and worshipped by the deluded heathen, or else they were purely figurative and allegorical. The gods could not be both 'good' and 'real'. On the other hand, Dante could not have believed in a merely figurative exist-ence of biblical characters. These theoretical hurdles and pitfalls are strewn all around our path once we venture into the scholastic hinterland (including Dante's own attempts at theory) but they are of less importance in the world of the *Commedia* owing to the unifying effect of allegory.

It is now widely recognized that allegory, far from being a kind of personal and private code or cryptography requir-ing a key supplied by the author,[2] was an imaginative habit shared by most cultivated people in medieval Europe. According to one highly typical mode utilized by Dante, a carefully selected object or event or facet of a situation was brought into focus and envisaged together with its meaning or meanings. For instance, the fable of Pyramus and Thisbe had the same general significance for Dante as for Ovid (roughly the equivalent of the Romeo and Juliet theme for modern times), but it ended with a visual symbol—the fruit of the mulberry stained with the hero's blood. This suggested various trains of thought but, however inter-preted, it was felt to sum up the true and deep meaning of the tale. We have here an example of the 'clear visual image' which is 'given much more intensity by having a

---

[1] T. S. Eliot, *Dante* (London, 1929), p. 32.

[2] For this view see Benedetto Croce, *La Poesia di Dante*, 2a ed. (Bari, 1921), p. 13.

meaning—we do not need to know what that meaning is, but in our awareness of the image we must be aware that the meaning is there too'.[1] Something of this attitude of mind was picked up, or so I hope to demonstrate in the course of this article, in the medieval schoolroom.

Allegory pursued in this and in countless other ways formed a common denominator for widely disparate domains of thought and experience. Biblical and pagan histories were seen in an identical perspective, and both, conceived as a storehouse of symbols, tended to compete in Dante's poetry with the 'real' world of known personages and recent events. I believe that this accounts for the peculiar concreteness and vividness of Dante's evocation of the gods—often presented by Dante in a way which seems utterly at variance with Virgil's bitter reference to the 'dei falsi e bugiardi': Dante speaks with enthusiastic approval of Apollo's flaying of Marsyas and with strong religious feeling of Glaucus' transformation into a marine deity. It accounts also for the tendency of mythological figures to multiply and proliferate and take the stage in some parts of the *Commedia* from the 'real life' characters.

If we attempt to list the characters really encountered by Dante, we find in the *Inferno* a long series of mythical and semi-human figures, unparalleled at any later stage in the poem;

CANTO

III	Charon	
V	Minos	
VI	Cerberus	
VII	Plutus	the only 'real' characters met and
VIII	Phlegyas	named in Cantos IV–IX are Ciacco
IX	Furies	(VI) and Filippo Argenti (VIII)
	Medusa	
XII	Minotaur	
	Centaurs	
	(Chiron	
	Nessus)	
XIII	Harpies	
XVI–XVII	Geryon	
XXV	Cacus	
XXXI	Giants	

[1] Eliot, pp. 22–23.

These are not poetic allusions (like the reference to Thebes and Troy in Canto xxx) but genuine encounters with localized beings who impede Dante's progress (Cerberus), speed him on his way (Geryon), or threaten him with annihiliation (Medusa). Their presence in the *Inferno* is fully justified by the medieval belief in demons and semi-human monsters: thanks to this belief Dante succeeds in introducing a large part of classical mythology as literal fact. But in the remainder of the *Commedia*, this is no longer possible: henceforth the corpus of pagan myth must perforce be presented in a more purely conceptual form—by visions, messages in the air, warning symbols on the rocks, poetic invocations or frankly metaphorical digressions by the poet speaking in his own person or through the mouth of one of his characters.

I shall attempt to show that, as is already plain from Moore's study of the sources, this entire corpus is Ovidian in origin, and moreover, that in designing his work Dante relied on the marginalia of the medieval manuscripts of Ovid in which the fables are presented from an allegorical angle. The Ovidian imagery emerges with startling and disturbing intensity in certain of the final cantos of the *Purgatorio* (xxvii–xxix and xxxii–xxxiii) and in the first five cantos of the *Paradiso*. In this small part of the work we find a dozen different Ovidian stories—about one-quarter of all the different stories from the *Metamorphoses* which are referred to in the *Commedia* as a whole. All of them have important symbolic values: Pyramus and Thisbe represent Dante's reunion with Beatrice, Phaeton's car the Chariot of the Church, Argus spiritual sight, Glaucus the mystery of divinization, Narcissus and the Bulls of Colchis the narrator's incredulity and wonderment at the heavens, the bloodstained mulberry the impurities which cloud his mind, the flaying of Marsyas divinely appointed suffering which is the gateway to the divine vision, the pursuit of Daphne by Apollo his own desire for poetic fame. The decorative frieze tends at this point to invade and take over the main design, since there is no succession of 'real-life' figures to challenge the attention, and most of the action is presented, if not by Ovidian imagery, in terms of Scriptural visions and dreams.

Another peculiar feature of the Ovidian myths in this section of the *Commedia* is that they are chosen from a wide range of the books of the *Metamorphoses*: Books I, III–VII, IX–X and XIII–XIV are all represented. It is worth while to inquire whether Dante attempted to complete the pattern by drawing on the remaining five books: in the later stages of the *Paradiso* he does in fact do so, since we can find scattered references to myths from Books II (Europa), VIII (Ariadne and Bacchus), XII (Leda and Gemini) and XV (Hippolytus), in Cantos xiii, xvii, and xxvii. The missing Book XI was probably represented by Orpheus (see the Appendix below, section XI). This is not accidental, since a similarly complete cycle of Ovidian myths covering all the fifteen books can be reconstructed from the *Inferno* and the central cantos of the *Purgatorio*, Cantos xii–xxv.

From this preliminary survey it appears that Ovidian myth was introduced in a variety of ways in the *Commedia*. A certain unity of treatment according to the allegorical mode of medieval poetry is continually threatened by the ambivalence of the medieval attitude to classical mythology. Yet the material itself is very carefully assembled and pieced together from the books of the *Metamorphoses*, and arranged in two great cycles, corresponding to the realm of Virgil and the realm of Beatrice. This distinction cuts clean across the existing tripartite division of the *Commedia*. I shall return to the structural implications of this at the end—but first I must deal in more detail with Dante's sources.

II

Practically all these myths were recognized as of Ovidian origin by Edward Moore in his monumental and in many respects definitive volume on Dante's scriptural and classical sources. Of the myths in the latter part of the *Inferno* he discussed the tales of Athamas and Ino and of Hecuba and Polydorus in his Ovid chapter, where he also adduced very subtle arguments to show that Dante knew of Nessus and Circe from Ovid; he drew attention to the debt of the transformation scene in *Inferno* xxv to Ovid's Hermaphroditus

INDEX OF THE OVIDIAN MYTHOLOGY IN THE *DIVINA COMMEDIA*

REALM OF VIRGIL

Inf.			Integ.
*v 4–15	Minos	IVc	201–2
*vi 13–33	Cerberus	IXc	361–2
*ix 37–51	Furies	IVc	199–200
*ix 52–57	Medusa	IV	229–30
*xii 11–27	Minotaur	VIIIa	321–4
xii 61–139	Nessus	IX	
*xii 70–72	Chiron	IIb	139–42
*xiii 10–15	Harpies	VIIa	295–6
*xvi–xvii	Geryon	IXa	357–8
xvii 106–8	Phaeton	II	
xvii 109–11	Icarus	VIII	
*xviii 83–87, 96	Jason	VIIb	297–302
xx 40–45	Tiresias	IIId	167–8
xxiv 106–11	Phoenix	XVa	
*xxv 17–33	Cacus	IXb	359–60
xxv 69–78	Hermaphroditus	IVb	193–4
xxv 97	*Cadmus*	III	153–6
xxv 97	*Arethusa*	V	273–4
xxvi 90–93	Circe	XIVb	475–8
xxix 58–64	Myrmidons	VIId	313–4
xxx 4–12	Athamas and Ino	IVd	213–14

REALM OF BEATRICE

Purg.			Integ.
xxvii 37–39	Pyramus and Thisbe	IVa	181–2
xxviii 49–51	Ceres and Proserpine	Vc	265–6
xxviii 64–66	Venus and Adonis	Xb	419–20
xxviii 139–44	*Golden Age*	*I*	
xxix 94–96	Argus	Ic	99–102
xxix 118–20	Phaeton and the Chariot of Phoebus	Id	111–14
xxxii 64–66	Argus and Mercury	Ic	99–102
xxxiii 46–51	*Themis' monster*	*VII*	
xxxiii 69	Pyramus	IVa	181–2

Par.			
*i 13–15, 31–33	Apollo and Daphne	Ib	93–96
i 20–21	Apollo and Marsyas	VIc	283–4
i 68–69	Glaucus	XIVa	469–74
ii 16–18	Jason and the Bulls	VIIc	299
iii 17–18	Narcissus	IIIb	163–4
iv 103–5	Alcmaeon and Eriphyle	IXd	389–90

xxx 13–21	Hecuba	XIIIb 457–8
xxx 37–42	Myrrha	Xa 413–14

Purg.

I 7–12	Calliope and Pierides	Vd 275–6
*xii 28–33	Giants	Ia 81–84
xii 37–39	Niobe	VIb 281–2
43–45	Arachne	VIa 277–8
xiv 139	Aglauros	IIc 147–50
xv 98	*Neptune and Minerva*	*VI* 279–80
xvii 19–21	Philomela and Procne	VId 289–90
xx 106–8	Midas	XIb 425–6
xx 115	*Polymestor*	*XIII*
xxi 130–2	*Latona on Delos*	*VI*
xxii 148–50	*Golden Age*	*I*
xxiii 22–27	Erysichthon	VIIId 337–8
xxiv 121–3	Centaurs	XIIa 445–8
xxv 22–24	Meleager	VIIIc 327–32
xxv 130–2	Diana and Helice	IIa 127–34

*v 70–72	Iphigenia	XIIIa
viii 67–70	*Typhoeus*	*V*
*xii 7–9	Muses—Sirens	Va, b 253–62
xii 14–15	Echo	IIIc 165–6
xiii 13–15, 25	Ariadne and Bacchus	VIIIb
xvii 1–3	*Phaeton and Climene*	*I*
xvii 46–47	Hippolytus	XVb 507–8
xxi 5–6	Semele	IIIa 159–62
xxvii 83–84	Europa	IId 151–2
* 98	Leda and Gemini	XIIb 449–52
xxxi 32–33	*Helice*	*II* 127–34

* Not attributed to the *Metamorphoses* by Moore.

Items italicized are additions to the cycle of 48 Ovidian myths discussed below; reference is added to the book of the *Meta-morphoses*. Myths belonging to this cycle are classified by the letters *a, b, c, d*, indicating their order within the book of the *Metamorphoses* or section of the *Integumenta*; see the Appendix for further details.

episode (see his paragraphs 5, 6, 7, 8, and 12). Almost
the complete series of Ovidian myths in the *Purgatorio* get
special mentions in this chapter (paragraphs 1, 2, 3, 4, 5,
15, 18, 19, 23, 24). For the *Paradiso* there is only one
important reference at the very end of the chapter (paragraph 31)—but it is clear from the Index to Quotations
that Moore had recognized almost the entire series of
mythical allusions from the *Metamorphoses* throughout the
Paradiso.

From Moore therefore the cycles can be reconstituted
almost in full—except for the monsters in the upper part of
Hell; we have seen that it is not easy to associate these with
the other Ovidian mythological references, usually aethereal
and allusive in tone, since these are characters whom Dante
meets 'in the flesh'. Whatever the reason, Moore preferred
to seek for the starting-point of these monsters in Virgil.
However, I propose to show that they are just as likely to
be Ovidian in origin as the others.

But Dante, contrary to what Moore supposed and all
commentators on Dante imply, did not obtain these references in the first place from the text of Ovid—the bare
text as we find it today in a Loeb or Teubner edition. A
thirteenth-century copy of the *Metamorphoses* was a com-
plicated affair:

The popularity of Ovid increased enormously in the thirteenth
century [says Ghisalberti]. The number of manuscripts traceable to
this century is considerable. But the point here is that they are covered
with traces of the study to which they were subjected. Few indeed are
the manuscripts of that age which lack glosses and commentary. A few
contain sporadic annotations in various hands, as we might expect;
for the *Metamorphoses* we can cite Paris, fonds latin 8000, 8002,
8197, 11314, 711. Others are provided with summaries and preceded
by an introduction, as in the famous Berneggerianus (twelfth century),
now lat. 8001. A very remarkable case is lat. 7993, a complete
thirteenth-century copy of Ovid (containing all his works except the
Ibis) without commentary—but with interlinear glosses and the
summaries of Lactantius Placidus for the *Metamorphoses* alone.
Others present a perpetual commentary enshrining the text in an
elaborate frame of encyclopedic glosses. Such codices are usually
provided with Lactantius' summaries of the stories, prefaced to each
book, or with the titles of Arnulf beginning: *Mutationes huius libri*

sunt hee. In one group of manuscripts these are found in a different form beginning: *Et in hoc volumine continetur.* In accord with scholastic tradition the anonymous commentator seeks to explain points of language and poetic syntax by an interlinear gloss which is in fact a piecemeal paraphrase in low Latin. The margins are reserved for various explanations, grammatical, geographical, astronomical, physical or more frequently historical and mythological, these being followed nearly always by mnemonic verses called *Integumenta* and prose allegories to which the medieval copyist seeks to draw attention by distinctive calligraphic signs.[1]

Of all these aids to study the most widespread in Dante's time may well have been the mnemonic poem in 520 lines in elegiac couplets called *Integumenta Ovidii*, now attributed to John of Garland (*c.* 1234), and the prose allegories of his predecessor, Arnulf of Orléans. These two works were generally interwoven, the prose and verse for each book being given together, with complete anonymity. Of the four relevant manuscripts in the Bodleian Library, all contain both the works together: one is a fourteenth-century copy of the *Metamorphoses*, with the works of Arnulf and John at the end of the book, the others are copies of the two commentaries alone.

It seems as if Dante knew these works throughout his life. Learned by rote at school, recurring in lectures and in the margins of manuscripts and in scholarly conversation, they must have lurked in the back of the mind of many literate people in the late thirteenth and fourteenth centuries. Although Moore and his successors (even during the thirty years since their publication by Ghisalberti) have ignored them, they played a more decisive part in the shaping of the mythological foundation of the *Commedia* than the text of Ovid himself.

Dante's indebtedness to this hitherto unexamined source can be best illustrated from cases where the Ovidian story used by Dante is framed in familiar formulae taken from the allegorical summaries and marginalia. The story of Hecuba and her children and of her final transformation into a dog is referred to thus in *Inf.* xxx:

[1] I translate from the introduction to *Integumenta Ovidii*, pp. 9–10.

BCED

> E quando la fortuna volse in basso
> L'altezza de' Troian che tutto ardiva
> Sì che insieme col regno il re fu casso,
>
> Ecuba trista, misera e cattiva
> Poscia che vide Polissena morta
> E del suo Polidoro in sulla riva
>
> Del mar si fu la dolorosa accorta,
> *Forsennata latrò si come cane,*
> *Tanto il dolor* le fe' la mente torta.   (13–21)

In the last two lines Dante is simply translating Arnulf: 'pre nimio dolore insanuit . . . sicut faciunt canes.' The medieval commentators with their usual rationalizing tendency assume that Hecuba *behaved* like a mad dog (that is, went mad) and was stoned like one, whereas Ovid gives a vivid description of her actual transmutation. Dante need scarcely have known the Ovidian passage: the whole history of Priam and his family as he gives it is told in a few lines of prose by his contemporary Giovanni del Virgilio in his *Allegoriae* in relation to this passage. The one point in common between Dante and Ovid is 'latrò' = 'latravit, conata loqui', *Met.* XIII.569 (she really barked).

The story of Athamas and Ino in the same canto is the neatest example of Dante's framing of Ovidian passages:

> *Atamante divenne tanto insano*
> Che veggendo la moglie con due figli
> Andar carcata da ciascuna mano,
>
> Gridò: 'Tendiam le reti si ch'io pigli
> La leonessa e i leoncini al varco:'
> E poi distese i dispietati artigli,
>
> Prendendo l'un che avea nome Learco,
> E rotollo, e percosselo ad un sasso,
> *E quella s'annegó con l'altro carco*   (4–12)

Evidently the middle terzina is based on Ovid, IV.513–14:

> Clamat 'io, comites, his retia tendite silvis!
> hic modo cum gemina visa est mihi prole leaena,'

and the account of the death of Learchus on 518–19:

> more rotat fundae, rigidoque infantia saxo
> discutit ora ferox.

But the opening line is simply a reminiscence of Arnulf: 'Ino et Athamas maritus eius de sanis facti sunt insani. Re vera quia deos contempnebant facti sunt insani. Nec mirum si maritus Inois factus sit insanus . . .' (note that *'divenne'* = *'factus est'*, as elsewhere); and the last line is curiously like a sentence in Giovanni del Virgilio: 'Ino dum esset ebria necuit se cum alio' (this sad story is attributed by the medievals partly to divine retribution and partly to drink: *'cum Ino interpretatur vinum'*).

A most curious instance of the marginalia providing Dante with a symmetrical epitome of Ovid is found in the stories of Niobe and Arachne:

> O Niobè, con che occhi dolenti
>   Vedeva io te segnata in sulla strada
>   Tra sette e sette tuoi figliuoli spenti!
>
> O Saul, come in sulla propria spada
>   Quivi parevi morto in Gelboe,
>   Che poi non senti pioggia nè rugiada!
>
> O folle Aragne, sì vedea in te
>   Già mezza aragna, trista in su gli stracci
>   Dell' opera che mal per te si fe'.
>
> O Roboam, già non par che minacci
>   Quivi il tuo segno; ma pien di spavento
>   Nel porta un carro prima che altri il cacci'
>   (*Purg.* xii.37–48)

Compare, in the *Integumenta*:

De Aragne	Ne quis maiori certet persuadet Aragne
	Que sub pauperie viscera viva trahit.
De nomine Athen-arum	Athanatos grecum sonat immortalis, Athenas
	Nominat hinc Pallas famaque vivit adhuc.
De Niobe	Proprietas saxi Niobe datur hoc quia durum,
	Hec quia dura riget firma tenore mali.
De sathiro	Certans cum Phebo satyrus notat insipientis
	Impar certamen cum sapiente trahi.

(277–284)

Dante has inverted the order of the two fables against pride, and substituted Old Testament figures for the intervening anecdotes (he makes an important use of one of these at a later stage: Marsyas, *Par.* i.19–21). Otherwise his terzinas are very similar in pattern to John of Garland's distichs. According to Moore, the link with Ovid is to be found in the explicit reference to *pride* as the cause of the heroines' downfall, and in the fact that Niobe has seven sons and seven daughters; he also cites:

> Orba resedit
> exanimes inter natos natasque virumque
> (VI.301–2)

as a close parallel with

> Tra sette e sette tuoi figliuoli spenti.

But both the features come straight from Arnulf: 'cum ipsa vii filios et vii filias haberet. Sed a filiis Latone vii filii Niobes et vii filie in simul ocisi sunt . . . Per Niobem habemus superbiam que vii filios habet . . . et vii filias.' No doubt Dante did have a vague memory of the Ovidian 'exanimes inter natos natasque'—but the whole structure and content of the passage come from the allegorists.

The allegorical marginalia frequently suggest the *angle* from which the Ovidian fable is approached by Dante. There are two mentions in the *Purgatorio* of the Pyramus legend, both linked with the entrance upon the scene of Beatrice:

> Come al nome di Tisbe aperse il ciglio
> Piramo in sulla morte, e riguardolla
> *Allor che il gelso diventò vermiglio* . . .
> (xxvii.37–39)

> E se stati non fossero acqua d'Elsa
> Li pensier vani intorno alla tua mente
> E il piacer loro *un Piramo alla gelsa* . . .
> (xxxiii.67–69)

There is no doubt that in writing the former passage Dante had Ovid's lines in mind:

> ad nomen Thisbes oculos a morte gravatos
> Pyramus erexit visaque recondidit illa
> (IV.145–6)

—and the quotation comes with supreme appropriateness at the moment when Dante is about to pass through the wall of flame in order to rejoin Beatrice. But why the recurrent reference to the mulberry (*gelso, gelsa*)? The discoloration of this fruit seems to have a profounder meaning for Dante than the central events of the fable—for Pyramus is alluded to by Beatrice not as 'the lover of Thisbe' but as 'the man who empurpled the mulberry'. This goes back to the *Integumenta*:

De morte Pirami   Alba prius morus nigredine mora colorans
                          Signat quod dulci mors in amore latet

(181–2)

—and Giovanni del Virgilio cites this couplet and develops the theme. The mulberry is the symbol of carnal love: *principio candet, fine negrescit*. Dante in these two allusive terzinas makes the fable a dual symbol, denoting his intense yearning for Beatrice and yet simultaneously the 'discoloration' of his mind which keeps him from her (he also restores the reddish-purple colour mentioned by Ovid in IV.127, where the allegorical commentators followed the dominant suggestion of blackish hue: 'in atram vertuntur faciem', 125–6, 'luctibus aptos semper habe fetus', 160–1).

The influence of the distichs is so pervasive that they may be assumed to play a part even when the epigrammatic line is already in Ovid. Thus with Glaucus:

di maris exceptum socio dignantur honore
(XIII.949)

—here is all Dante needed to create his tremendous image of the transforming union with the divine:

Qual si fe' Glauco nel gustar dell' erba
Che il fe' consorte in mar degli altri Dei.
(*Par.* i.68–69)

But would Dante have noticed this line without his long acquaintance with the marginalia where the idea was *monté en épingle*? (See the texts cited in the Appendix, section XIV.)

The most striking case of Dante's synoptic reading of text and gloss is to be found in his references to Helice:

Al bosco
Si tenne Diana ed Elice caccionne;
(*Purg.* xxv.130–1)

Se i Barbari, venendo da tal plaga
Che ciascun giorno d'Elice si copra,
Rotante col suo figlio ond' ell' è vaga . .
(*Par.* xxxi.31–33)

Here, in his last satiric fling at the Florentines ('from earth to heaven, from barbarian North to Rome, and away from Florence among decent people') Dante suddenly introduces the rare name *Helice* for the Bear, whereas previously he has always referred to 'il Carro' or 'l'Orse'. It is still more puzzling how he came to apply the name to the nymph whom Diana banished from the wood—for Ovid gives her no name, and further research in other works of Ovid (see *Fasti*, ii.153–92) and other Latin poets is likely to produce the name *Callisto*. The name *Helice* for the constellation is also found in the *Fasti* (iii.107–8, iv.575–80), whence the identification with Callisto can be inferred. But it is the allegorists and not Dante who were acquainted at first-hand with these texts, and his immediate source lies to hand in the *Integumenta*:

	Arcticus ex arcto polus est regione gelata
	Stella caret casu vim gerit ursa gelu.
De Calistone	Arcadie domina Calisto dicitur ursa
vel seculis	Nam gravidata Iovis semine turpis erat.
nauticis	Ursa tibi maior Elice dicetur et Artos
	Sed Cinosura sequens dicitur Ursa minor
	Plaustri languentis hec est auriga Bootes
	Et custos matris est Cinosura sue.

(127–134)

This gloss not only provides five names for the Great Bear (Callisto, Helice, Ursa Maior, Arctos, Plaustrum) and two for the Little Bear (Cynosura, Ursa Minor), but summarizes Ovid's fable in a distich and places the whole interlocking set of explanations in the margin of Ovid's text. The important point is not just that Dante knew all this astronomic and mythological lore—but that he had always known it, from his schooldays, or from whatever later period he began the serious study of Ovid, that he knew it by heart in close relation to a specific Ovidian myth, that of Diana and Callisto.

So far we have considered cases where reflections of Ovid and of the allegories are combined—but there are cases even more numerous where Dante need not have consulted or remembered the actual text of Ovid at all. To write his single line:

> Io sono Aglauro che divenni sasso
> (*Purg.* xiv.139)

and place it in the warnings against Envy, he needed only the four words of the *Integumenta*:

> Aglauros invida facta lapis (150)

(note here again 'facta [sum] = 'divenni'). It is perhaps even more obvious that to write

> Taccia di Cadmo e d'Aretusa Ovidio
> (*Inf.* xxv.97)

he needed only chapter headings such as Arnulf's Arethusa 'nimpha in linpham'. The choice of words often reveals a debt to the medieval gloss, thus the conjunction of the adjectives 'avarus' and 'miser' in the marginal distich on Midas is reflected in

> E la miseria dell' avaro Mida.
> (*Purg.* xx.106)

Ovid once refers to Midas as 'wealthy and miserable' ('divesque miserque', XI.127), but he does not call him 'avarus'; Midas is for him an example not of avarice but of general stupidity (asking the gods for the wrong thing). No doubt it was the association of the two epithets in the medieval schoolroom that engendered the peculiar semantic development of the word 'miser' in English. Again the striking opening of the distichs on Meleager

> Fax est fatalis Meleagri perdere fortis ..   (327)

is more likely to have suggested

come Meleagro
Si consumò al consumar d'un stizzo
            (*Purg.* xxv. 22–23)

than the lengthy Ovidian account in which the fatal object is more often referred to as a billet ('stipes') or branch
('ramus') than as a flaming brand ('torris', VIII.457 [var.
'ramus'], 512).[1] Perhaps, however, the most revealing of
Dante's debts to the forgotten John of Garland is to be
found in the latter's allegorization of Apollo's pursuit of
Daphne as the scholar's pursuit of fame:

> Mentibus hec arbor sapientum virgo virescit
> Que quamvis fugiat victa labore viret:
> Est virgo Phebi sapientia facta corona
> Laurus, quam cupida mente requirit homo.   (93–96)

Ghisalberti points out that this is an entirely original
interpretation on the part of John of Garland (for Arnulf and

---

[1] The description of the six-winged creatures in the vision of *Purg.* xxix:
> Ognuno era pennuto di sei ali,
>   Le penne *piene d'occhi;* e gli occhi d'Argo
>   Se fosser vivi sarebber cotali   (94–96)

contains an echo of *Integumenta* 99: 'Argus ab arguto fertur qui plenus
ocellis. . . .' The reference to the vengeance of Calliope on the Pierides:
> E qui Calliopè alquanto surga
> Seguitando il mio canto con quel suono . . .
>   (*Purg.* i. 9–10)

presents difficulty: Moore cites 'surgit et inmissos hedera collecta capillos
Calliope' (V. 338–9), but this is some hundreds of lines from the climax
of the contest, which contains the more significant passage:
> Finierat dictos e nobis maxima cantus;
> at nymphae vicisse deas Helicona colentes
> *concordi dixere sono.* (662–4)

Dante may have taken this to imply that the nymphs accompanied Calliope's
song, just as he asks her to accompany his. But in any case Dante knew the
commentators' equation: 'Calliope' = (optimus) sonus'. The allusion in
Par. xii.7–8:
> Canto che tanto vince nostre Muse,
>   Nostre Sirene, in quelle dolci tube . . .

arises from the joint treatment of the Muses and Sirens in the allegorists:
Calliope is said to be the mother of the Sirens, the three sirens stand for music
made by voices, wind instruments and strings respectively: 'voce,' 'tuba',
'cithara' (see the passages cited in the Appendix, section V).

Giovanni del Virgilio, the myth is concerned with virginity and the pursuit of virginity, which is only permanent and immutable in the next world), and there is little doubt that Dante had this in mind when he wrote *Par.* i.13–15 (the fate of Marsyas there alluded to is likewise prominent in the allegorical marginalia).

It remains to mention a few cases which are not usually regarded as Ovidian either directly or indirectly. Cacus as a Centaur no doubt derives from a misunderstanding of Virgil's *Semihominis Caci*. But, although Cacus does not appear in the *Metamorphoses*, Dante's placing of him among the thieves must owe something to the glaring medieval sub-titles of Book ix:

> De Caco   Cacus latro fuit. . . .   (359)

where Cacus appears between Geryon and Cerberus among the monsters slain by Hercules. It was from the schoolroom allegories that Dante learned that Niobe and Arachne symbolized Pride, Aglauros Envy, Midas Avarice and Cacus Theft; and so the imposing structure of the *Commedia* began to form half unawares in the recesses of his mind. There is no need to look any farther for the origins of Geryon and Cerberus; Geryon is completely transformed by Dante without further assistance from the classics, but the 'sop to Cerberus' does of course derive from *Aen.* vi.417–23. The horrific apparition of the Three Furies in *Inferno*, ix, is another instance of the 'framing' of classical poetic allusions in schoolbook mnemonics:

> Tre furie infernal di sangue tinte . . .

> Questa è Megera dal sinistro canto,
>   Quella che piange dal destro è Aletto,
>   Tesifone è nel mezzo . . .   (38, 46–48)

The central lines of this passage are a wondrous imitation of Statius, *Thebaid*, i.103–15, but the framework is simply the medieval caption and distich;

> De tribus furiis   Mentes verba manus sordent, Alecto flagellat
>   inferni   Mentes, Thesiphone verba, Megera manus.
>   (199–200)

There seems no good reason to doubt that the remaining monsters and demi-gods of the Upper Hell first came Dante's way in the marginalia to Ovid, although in a few cases (the Harpies in the Suicides' Wood, cf. *Aen.* iii.22–48, 209–69) they owe a deeper and nobler poetic resonance to the contact with Virgil.

III

The debt which Dante owes to the allegorical distichs and prose summaries is obviously considerable, both in the detail and in the structure of his poem. They help to account for the brevity of his style, just as the allegorical modes account for the sharpness of his visual imagery. It is ironical that the nineteenth-century commentators who praised 'the fresh touches by which he shows the very heart of the story' (Moore quoting Dr. Carlyle, with reference to Athamas and Ino) never sought their origin in the unassuming school texts of which copies were to be found in the Bodleian and in the margins of late-medieval manuscripts of Ovid. They are Dante's heritage from the schoolmen, in the old, unpretentious sense of the word; over and over again, his lapidary simplicity and concision derives from their pedagogic signposts and headlines and sub-titles. Dante's gods are to a large extent the 'gods of the copy-book headings'.

But not entirely—for Dante did not go the whole way with his schoolmasters or even with his acquaintances in the humanist vanguard like Giovanni del Virgilio. These commentators were extraordinarily rationalistic, but it is only rarely that Dante catches their tone in this respect. Moore comments on the 'curiously rationalistic treatment of the myth of Typhoeus, where Dante says that the volcanic phenomena of Sicily are due to the presence of sulphur and not to the struggles of the buried Typhoeus':

> non per Tifeo ma per nascente solfo
> (*Par.* viii.70)

This is very like Giovanni del Virgilio, v.13: 'Sed quod sit sub Ethna, hoc est solum similitudinarie, quia Ethna est mons Sicilie ignem vomens, quare dicunt Typheum ibi

esse. Et eodem modo intellige de similibus'. The allegorists
carried this 'eodem modo de similibus' to its logical and
risible extreme. Many of the myths have physical explanations: Phoebus is the sun's heat, Clymene moisture,
Phaeton the crops, and the earth is scorched in the autumn
when the crops are harvested; the staining of the mulberry
is simply the change of colour as the fruit ripens. Pasiphae
loved a notary employed by Minos who was called Taurus
and bore twins who were known collectively as the *Mino-*
taurus; the belief that the Minotaur was a monster indicates
reprobation of her adultery. Europa went to sea in a ship
which had a bull painted on it, or else the ship's name was
'Bull'. As for the divinization of Glaucus, the herb caused
Glaucus the fisherman to plunge into the ocean—whence
the deluded heathen believing in marine deities assumed
that he had been transformed into one, 'unde fingitur esse
mutatus in deum marinum'.[1] Dante will have none of this.
His Minotaur is an entirely bull-like creature:

> Qual è quel toro che si slaccia in quella
>   Che ha ricevuto già'l colpo mortale ..
>   (*Inf.* xii.22–23)

Glaucus really ate the herb and became a consort of the
marine deities ('Qual si fe' Glauco . . . Che il fe' consorte');
his experience does not measure up to the reality of divinization, but it is itself something more than words and not
simply a figure of speech:

> Trasumanar significar *per verba*
>   Non si poria; pero l' esempio basti .
>   (*Par.* i.70–71).

It is a mark of Dante's greatness that he passes clean over
these timid explanations (so reminiscent of the *libre penseur*
teaching the village children that 'Jeanne d'Arc crut
entendre des voix'), and thus prepares the way for a fuller
imaginative revival of the ancient Pantheon in the early
Florentine renaissance.

These researches tend to diminish very considerably the

---

[1] See Ghisalberti's article on Arnulf, pp. 195–7, for scores of similar
examples.

amount of direct contact with the Ovidian text implied by
the numerous references to the *Metamorphoses* in our
current editions of the *Commedia*, and to place such contacts
as there really are in a subtly different light. Apart from the
odd lines and passages which I have already cited, Dante
certainly made a skilful use of the episode of Nessus at the
ford (IX.101–33) and the transformation of Hermaphroditus (IV.365–79) and of Tiresias (III.324–31). This is
practically all for the *Inferno*. In the *Purgatorio*, apart from
odd lines already cited, there is the description of Fames
(VIII.801–4, 825) applied to the sinners fasting in the
sixth cornice, the allusion to Proserpine's spring flowers
(V.391–401) and the wry use made of VII.759–65:

> Carmina Laiades non intellecta priorum
> solverat ingeniis . . .
>
> protinus Aoniis inmittitur altera Thebis
> pestis et exitio multi pecorumque suoque . . .

where Dante's text read *Naiades* for *Laiades* 'son of Laius,
Oedipus'. There is little to record for the *Paradiso* except
stray phrases (XIII.949, VII.118–21, II.868–9). To
these we must add the description of the Golden Age (I.
89–112) and a number of imperfectly remembered phrases
reflected here and there in Dante's verse (see Moore, pp.
222–7)—all in all, less than a dozen passages from the
Metamorphoses which have been intentionally and clearly
imitated, out of nearly seventy allusions to this work in
Moore's Index of Quotations. On the other hand there are
at least four very likely allusions to the *Heroides*:

> Ma Ellesponto . . .
>
> Più odio da Leandro non sofferse,
>   Per mareggiare intra Sesto ed Abido
>   (*Purg.* xxviii.71–74)
>
> Nè quella Rodopeia che delusa
>   Fu da Demofoonte; nè Alcide
>   Quando Iole nel cor ebbe richiusa . . .
>   (*Par.* ix.100–2)
>
> Ivi con segni e con parole ornate
>   Isifile ingannò, la giovinetta
>   (*Inf.* xviii.91–92)

and the recurrent references to the veracity of dreams at daybreak (*Inf.* xxvi.7, *Purg.* ix.16–18). There are one or two allusions to Ovid's treatises on love. The point is of some importance, since the *Heroides*, a very popular work in the fourteenth century (it was soon to be translated into Greek prose), seems to have been a formative influence on Dante, suggesting the extensive use of prosopopeia which was to be the dominant literary device of the *Commedia*. If Dante in his early years knew classical myth and allusion largely from epigrams, summaries, and 'helps to study', it is important to realize that his tastes may have led him to browse more widely once his enthusiasm for classical poetry was fully aroused. If it is erroneous to refer to the text of the *Metamorphoses* for every mythological allusion in the *Commedia*, it is equally misleading to suppose that Dante, when he came to read Ovid more fully, confined himself to this one work.

IV

We can now return to the structural problem already briefly suggested at the beginning of this article. It is plain that Dante worked out a carefully organized plan of Ovidian myths with John of Garland in front of him or vividly present in his memory. But it is equally plain that the Ovidian cycles so laid out by Dante do not correspond very closely to the tripartite pattern of the *Commedia* in its final form. There are certain unescapable facts: some of the myths are embodied in passages full of sharp visual detail borrowed from the actual text of Ovid or Statius, while others have been left in the state of laconic allusions. Some parts of the finished poem are far more deeply Ovidian than others (there is practically nothing to cite for *Purg.* i-xii and very little for the latter half of the *Paradiso*), without any apparent reason for this uneven distribution of the mythical allusions. Here we are on the fringes of speculation. It might be reasonable to assume that the two great cycles of myth which persist in the extant text were drafted very early, perhaps about 1306, and that they express the author's new-found enthusiasm for ancient poetry and the profound urge which he then felt to express the truths of

religion in Ovidian symbolism. Later, as the poem came to
be rehandled and large parts of it finished, in the harsh
years after 1313, the old mood had passed. New tastes and
interests supervened. Dante no longer wished to develop the
Ovidian content of his poem, but he left large parts of his
existing work more or less *in situ* within the larger context
which he had devised.

The pattern of borrowings from the allegorists seems to
relate to an embryonic stage of Dante's great design, when
the poet was still hesitating between a bipartite and a
tripartite structure, neither of which corresponds exactly
to the poem in three cantiche which was bequeathed to
posterity:

I		II
REALM OF VIRGIL		REALM OF BEATRICE
Hell *Intermediate States*		*Earthly Paradise and*
(semi-human figures: sinners		*the Heavens*
still unadmitted to beatitude;		
others whose fate remains in		
doubt; &c.)		

1	2	3
Inf.	*Purg.* xii–xxv	*Purg.* xxvii to end,
		Paradiso (in
		embryo)

It might seem that when Dante came to draw up his list of
forty-eight myths, he had not finally decided to develop the
purgatory as a large, independent unit. It is scarcely
possible to believe, in view of the unity of tone, the intensely
Ovidian imagery and the dominating presence of Beatrice
throughout *Purg.* xxvii to *Par.* iii, that he had yet detached
the earthly paradise from the remaining spheres of beatitude
to which it forms an introduction; and perhaps he had not
yet designed the ante-purgatory at all. Nor is this possibility
at all surprising if we consider the background of medieval
visionary literature. There is probably no example before
Dante of an other-world voyage in which Hell and Purgatory are as sharply separated as they are in the *Divina
Commedia*. In the *Visio Tundali* both regions lie close together below the earth's surface; for the Celtic visionary
we might say that purgatory was only one specialized aspect

of the mystery of divinely imposed suffering which he is permitted to glimpse. He finds upon his path many sufferers whose pains are mitigated or cease altogether at certain stated times, either because of some good deeds which they performed, or through the intercession of a heavenly being. There was always room in these apocalyptic visions for intermediary states, such as that of the angels who fell not from pride or malice but out of a mistaken loyalty to Lucifer, their one-time leader. The creation of an open-air purgatory under the stars is one of Dante's most brilliant strokes; and no doubt he had always envisaged within his plan a special training ground, where souls destined for bliss were exercised in resistance to the seven sins. But it is possible, indeed I think likely, that his original conception was more traditional, that his corrective training could have taken place in an annexe to the main gaol, and that in this context the final destiny of some souls could be left in doubt.

If we are willing to consider this bipartite plan as at any rate a possibility existing at various times in Dante's mind during his shaping of the *Commedia*, an important confirmation can be found in the division of the whole of Dante's journey between two guides, Virgil and Beatrice. How is it, one wonders, that Virgil who can never himself enjoy the divine vision, climbs out into the starlit slopes of purgatory and converses blithely with many Christian souls destined for bliss? Is not this a proof of some interconnexion between the two realms, which remain utterly distinct from the earthly paradise? There is another vital clue in the invocations to the Muses and Apollo which now figure in the first cantos of the *Purgatorio* and the *Paradiso* respectively:

> Ma qui la morta poesì resurga
> O sante Muse, poichè vostro sono,
> E qui Calliopè alquanto surga,

> Seguitando il mio canto con quel suono
> De cui le Piche misere sentiro
> Lo colpo tal, che disperar perdono.
> *(Purg.* i.7–12)

> O buono Apollo, all' ultimo lavoro
> Fammi del tuo valor si fatto vaso,
> Come domandi a dar l'amato alloro.
>
> Infino a qui l'un giogo di Parnaso
> Assai mi fu, ma or con ambedue
> M'è uopo entrar nell' aringo rimaso.
>
> Entra nel petto mio, e spira tue
> Sì come quando Marsia traesti
> Della vagina delle membra sue.
>
> *(Par.* i.13–21)

These passages present a remarkable degree of parallelism: in each the poet addresses a pagan divinity and asks for help in his task (to revive the lost art of poetry, to win the laurel crown), and in each he accompanies this with a commemoration of a naked act of power by which the divinity vindicated his or her claims in the face of impious denial by mortals. Clearly they are well fitted to introduce two complementary parts of the work. But in detail they seem strangely unfitted to their present position. Why preface the *Purgatorio*, in which everyone is assured of final salvation, with a reference to those who 'despaired of pardon'? And why the *Paradiso* with a palmary instance of divinely imposed suffering (expressed by a peculiarly horrifying symbol) just at the moment when we have left the realm of suffering entirely? Each invocation, instead of stating the theme of the cantica to which it is prefaced, refers back to a preceding one. But everything would be in order if these invocations were prefaced to the 'realm of Virgil' and the 'realm of Beatrice' respectively. The story of the Pierides would serve as a gentle warning to those who struggle against the divine supremacy, for herein lies the parting of the ways leading to Hell or Purgatory. The flaying of Marsyas might seem (and probably does seem to most readers) a mere grotesque decoration, but what was it in Dante's intention? Did he accept the allegorists' interpretation of it as the triumph of wisdom over folly? Or does it merely serve to underline the power of his patron Apollo, giver of the coveted laurel? Dante's practice elsewhere suggests that the flaying was meant to be fully

realized, like the transformation of Glaucus and the staining
of the mulberry, as a genuinely awesome *event* containing
in itself some further significance. If it meant, as for the
early renaissance Platonists, divinely willed purgation, then
it would come appropriately *before* (not *after*) the episode
of the sheet of flame, through which the terrified traveller
must pass, despite the recoil of his physical nature, in order
to rejoin Beatrice and ascend to the blessed realm.

These arguments in favour of an early bipartite plan are
confirmed in detail by the extant pattern of Ovidian myth,
seen in relation to its source-book, the *Integumenta*. Dante,
using John of Garland's distichs and sub-headings, assembled from books I–IX of the *Metamorphoses* nine groups
of three myths which he distributed evenly between Hell,
the intermediate state and Paradise, thus:

	Hell	Intermediate State	Paradise
I			3
II		3	
III			3
IV	3		
V			3
VI		3	
VII	3		
VIII		3	
IX	3		

The structure of these groups is often clearly visible in the
text of John of Garland himself, thus:

Bk. II	De Calistone vel			(a)
	seculis nauticis	(Elice)		
	De Erictonio			
	De Coronide et corvo			
	De Ochiroe, Chirone,			(b)
	Esculapio			
	De omnibus hiis qui			(c)
	mutabantur in saxum	(Aglauros)		
Bk. III	De Bacho	Deceptam Semelem . . .		(a)
	De Narciso	Narcisus puer . . .		(b)
		Dicitur in silvis Echo		(c)

THE FORTY-EIGHT OVIDIAN MYTHS ARRANGED IN THE ORDER OF THE ALLEGORISTS

	REALM OF VIRGIL		REALM OF BEATRICE
	Hell	*Intermediate States*	*Earthly Paradise and Heaven*
I		Giants smitten by Jove	Apollo and Daphne—Argus and Mercury—Phaeton and the Chariot of the Sun
II		Diana and Helice—Chiron—Aglauros	Europa and the Bull
III	Tiresias		
IV	Hermaphroditus and Salmacis—Furies and Minos—Athamas and Ino		Semele—Narcissus—Echo / Pyramus and Thisbe
V		Calliope and the Pierides	Muses—Sirens—Ceres and Proserpine
VI		Arachne—Niobe—Philomela and Procne	Apollo and Marsyas
VII	Harpies—Jason and Medea—Myrmidons		Jason ploughing with the Bulls of Colchis
VIII		Minotaur—Meleager—Erysichthon	Ariadne
IX	Geryon—Cacus—Cerberus		Alcmaeon and Eriphyle
X	Myrrha		Venus and Adonis
XI		Midas	Orpheus
XII		Centaurs and Lapithi	Leda and Gemini
XIII	Hecuba		Iphigenia
XIV	Circe and Ulysses		Glaucus
XV	Phoenix		Hippolytus and Phaedra

Bk. IX	De Gerione	Triplex Gerionis caput . . .	(a)
	De Caco	Cacus latro fuit . . .	(b)
	De Cerbero	Cerberus est mundus . . .	(c)

In each case the group of three myths was attributed as a whole to one particular part of the poem, and this arrangement is still visible in the extant text, provided that we accept (*a*) that the earthly paradise is grouped with the *Paradiso* and (*b*) that Chiron and the Minotaur were originally placed, as half-human creatures not meriting absolute salvation or damnation, in the intermediate state.

So far the distribution of the myths implies a tripartite plan—but Dante did not pursue this. To complete his borrowings from the *Metamorphoses* he now groups Hell and the intermediate regions together as the 'realm of Virgil', adding one myth from each book which was not previously represented either in the 'realm of Virgil' or the 'realm of Beatrice' as the case might be, in such a way that four myths are drawn from each of the first nine books of Ovid and distributed in the proportions 3 : 1 or 1 : 3 between the two realms. For the remaining books X–XV he chooses one myth for each realm from each book, thus:

| | REALM OF VIRGIL | | REALM OF BEATRICE | |
	Hell	*Intermediate States*	*Paradise*	*Total*
I		1	3	4
II		3	1	4
III	1		3	4
IV	3		1	4
V		1	3	4
VI		3	1	4
VII	3		1	4
VIII		3	1	4
IX	3		1	4
X	1		1	2
XI		1	1	2
XII		1	1	2
XIII	1		1	2
XIV	1		1	2
XV	1		1	2
	14 +1	12	21	48

Additions to the above pattern of Ovidian myths in the extant text are generally trivial (see the italicized elements in the Index of Ovidian Mythology on pp. 6–7 above).

Everything I have said in the last few pages depends on two assumptions: that the subtle web of relationships linking the fifteen books of the *Metamorphoses* with the two 'realms' of the *Commedia* is due to design, not chance; and that if Dante selected and arranged his Ovidian material with so much care, he must have had in mind a poem of congruent structure (which the extant *Commedia* is not).

Either assumption can be challenged or rejected, and to do this would be to undermine the deductions which I have made from them. Attempts to invalidate them might lead to further research and unexpected discoveries. But if my arguments in favour of an early bipartite form of the poem retain any validity, the conclusion we must draw is that Dante began as an Ovidian singer of a Celtic underworld, a Christian Orpheus who had returned from the world of shades, but that finally he lost interest in Ovid altogether.[1] His work as he first designed it might not have differed very much in tone from many symbolic and mythological poems of the fourteenth century. But after 1313 new ambitions came to the fore: Virgil became the master and guide and leader. The geography of the underworld was elaborated and purgatory emerged as a separate realm. Dante wrote in the political prophecies and denunciations, and, by linking the poem with his own destiny and that of his 'humble Italy', became the singer of his country's past and future, while his simple sketch based on Celtic visions and schoolroom Ovid was transformed into the sacred poem to which heaven and earth had lent their aid.

---

[1] In the process the figure of Orpheus himself has been eliminated from the *Paradiso*. This is an absolutely unique case where the myth required to fill out the plan of borrowings from the fifteen books is missing from the extant *Commedia* (see Appendix, section XI).

THE FORTY-EIGHT OVIDIAN MYTHS ARRANGED IN THE HYPOTHETICAL ORDER OF DANTE'S EARLY DRAFT

REALM OF VIRGIL
Invocation of Calliope punishing the Pierides (divine retribution on the unrepentant)

REALM OF BEATRICE
Invocation of Apollo (a) pursuing Daphne (poetic fame), (b) flaying Marsyas (acceptance of divinely imposed suffering)

Hell

Inf.
- vi   Cerberus (Gate of Hell)
- ix   Minos and Furies (Judgement)
-       Athamas and Ino ⎱ (Violence)
- xiii Hecuba ⎰
- xiii Harpies
- xvii Geryon (Fraud)
- xviii Jason (Seduction)
- xx   Tiresias (Sorcery)
- xxiv Phoenix (The Resurrection of the Body)
- xxv   Cacus (Theft) ⎱
-       Hermaphroditus ⎰ (Deception)
- xxvi Circe
- xxix Myrmidons
- xxx   Myrrha

Intermediate States

Purg.
-        Chiron
-        Minotaur
- xii   Giants ⎱ (Pride)
-        Niobe
-        Arachne ⎰
- xiv   Aglauros (Envy)
- xvii   Philomela and Procne (Wrath)
- xx   Midas (Avarice)
- xxiii Erysichthon ⎱ (Gluttony)
- xxiv   Centaurs ⎰
- xxv   Meleager (Union of soul and body)
-        Diana and Helice (Unchastity)

Earthly Paradise

Purg.
- xxvii Pyramus and Thisbe (Reunion with Beatrice)
- xxviii Proserpine (Innocence)
-        Venus (Beauty)
- xxix   Phaeton (The Chariot of the Church)
- xxix   Argus ⎱ (Vision)
- xxxii ⎰

The Heavens

Par.
- i   Glaucus (Divinization)
- ii   Jason and the Bulls (Wonder)
- iii   Narcissus (Sight of the Blessed)
- iv   Alcmaeon ⎱ (Conflict of duties)
- v   Iphigenia ⎰
- xii   Muses—Sirens—Echo (Music of Heaven)
- xiii   Ariadne (Blessed as constellations)
-        Orpheus (The poet's vision of the underworld)
- xvii   Hippolytus (His exile for duty's sake)
- xxi   Semele (Fire of the Blessed)
- xxvii Europa ⎱ (Blessed as constellations)
-        Leda and Gemini ⎰

Appendix

THE FORTY-EIGHT OVIDIAN MYTHS ACCORDING TO JOHN OF GARLAND, WITH ILLUSTRATIVE EXTRACTS FROM ARNULF OF ORLÉANS AND GIOVANNI DEL VIRGILIO

I

(a) De malicia
    gigantum

Eiecisse deos mundus sitit. Inde ruinam
    Primus habet, virtus mentis ab arce fugit:
Virtutes Superi, viciorum turba Gigantes,
    Mens humilis Phlegra, mons tibi fastus erit.
    (81–84)

(b) De Phebo et
    Dane

Mentibus hec arbor sapientum virgo virescit
    Que quamvis fugiat victa labore viret:
Est virgo Phebi sapientia facta corona
    Laurus, quam cupida mente requirit homo.
    (93–96)

(c) De Argo

Argus ab arguto fertur qui plenus ocellis
    Ante retro, plena calliditate sapit:
Cauda pavonis tandem pinguntur ocelli
    Quando divicias despicit argus homo.
    (99–102)

(d) De Phetone[1]

Phos lux dicetur et Pheton dicitur inde
    Sic splendor solis filius esse potest:
Philosophi radium generat sapientia cuius
    Currum deducit, sed cadit arte rudis.
    (111–14)

II

(a)

Articus ex arcto polus est regione gelata
    Stella caret casu vim gerit ursa gelu.

De Calistone
vel seculis
nauticis.

Arcadie domina Calisto dicitur ursa
    Nam gravidata Iovis semine turpis erat.
Ursa tibi maior Elice dicetur et Artos

---

[1] The story of Phaeton and the chariot of the Sun occurs in *Met.* II, and in Book II of Arnulf and Giovanni del Virgilio, but is treated at the end of I by John of Garland.

Sed Cinosura sequens dicitur Ursa minor.
Plaustri languentis hec est auriga Bootes
Et custos matris est Cinosura sue.
(127–34)

(b) De Ochiroe,   Ochiroe Chiron heros epidaurius usum
  Chirone,   Corpore mortis habet vivere scire datur:
  Esculapio   Pars hominis ratio est, pars sordet equina
         cadaver,
      Pars ratione carens, pars aditura solum.
(139–42)

(c) De omnibus hiis   Vir valet invictus et inexorabilis esse
  qui mutabantur   Saxum, nam lapidem pectore durus habet.
  in saxum   Mens domus Invidie, Pallas sapientia, sermo
      Aliger, Aglauros invida facta lapis.
(147–50)

  Cf. Arnulf:
  Aglauros invida Mercurium volens expellere mutata est in
  lapidem . . . (ii. 12)

(d) De Europa[1]   Iupiter Europam rapuit rate, taurus in illa
      Pictus erat, taurus nomine navis erat.
(151–2)

III

(a) De Bacho   Deceptam Semelem corpus dic esse solutum
      Quod gula dissolvit flammaque cara meri.
      Sunt gemine matres duplex natura falerni
       Cui pater est estas, humida mater hiems.

(b) De Narciso   Narcisus puer est cupidus quem gloria rerum
      Fallit que florent que velut umbra fluunt.

(c)   Dicitur in silvis Echo regnare quod illic
      Aer inclusus verba referre solet.

(d) De Tiresia   Vir modo Tiresias modo femina dicitur esse
      Quorum natura notificatur ei.
(159–68)

IV

(a) De morte Pirami   Alba prius morus nigredine mora colorans
      Signat quod dulci mors in amore latet.
(181–2)

---

[1] Placed at the beginning of III by John of Garland.

Cf. Arnulf:

> Mora de albis in nigra nichil aliud est quam quod alba sunt nondum matura, sed nigrescunt dum maturescunt.
>
> (iv.4)

Cf. Giovanni del Virgilio:

> Quarta transmutatio est de moris que de albis versa sunt in nigra. Nam verum est quod morus prius producit mora alba, deinde cum sunt matura efficiuntur nigra. Moraliter ergo per hoc possumus notare quod in amore qui est dulcis in principio aliquando mors latet, quia ad ipsum sepe consequitur mors sicut consecutum fuit in istis duobus. U. v.:

> Alba prius morus nigredine mora colorans
> Signat quod dulci mors in amore latet.
> Tincta suos fetus de sanguine mortis amantum,
> Principio candet fine nigrescit arbor. (iv.4)

(b) De fonte Salmacis — Cellula matricis fons fertur Salmacis in qua Infans conceptus hermafroditus erit.

(193–4)

(c) De tribus furiis inferni — Mentes verba manus sordent, Alecto flagellat Mentes, Thesiphone verba, Megera manus.

De tribus iudicibus inferni — Mens Minos, vox est Radamantus et Eacus actus

Tres sunt et torquent crimina trina reis.

(199–202)

(d) De Inone submersa — Ino submersa moritur, dire lapidescunt, Et volucrum cetus est fugitiva cohors.

(213–14)

Cf. Arnulf:

> Ino et Athamas maritus eius de sanis facti sunt insani. Re vera quia deos contempnebant facti sunt insani. Nec mirum si maritus Inois factus sit insanus, cum Ino interpretatur vinum . . . (iv.15)

Cf. Giovanni del Virgilio:

> Vigesima est de Athamante et Inoe. Verum fuit quod Athamas rex Thebarum et Ino dum colerent Bachum inebriati sunt. Quapropter Juno i. voluntas dei et actio voluit eos punire. Unde Athamas ebrius occidit unum ex filiis. Ino dum esset ebria necuit se cum alio . . . (iv.20)

V

(a) De Musis sicut   Hec tibi succurrit dircei concio fontis:
    habetur in com-   Historico meditans carmina Clio pede,
    pendio auc-   Euterpeque tuba clangens, memoransque
    torum   remota
                    Melpomene, ridens sponte Talia iocos,
             Tersicore cum psalterii modulamine campum
                    Intrat, adest Eratho res reperire potens,
             Verba polire venit edocta Polimnia, stellas
                    Uranie numerat hiisque futura notat,
             Calliopeque movet citharam mellitaque voicis
                    Organa sollicitat letificatque coros.

                                      (253–62)

(b)   Cf. Arnulf:
         Sirenes filie Acheloi et Calliroes fuerunt bene cantantes . . .
         ideo dicitur Caliope mater earum esse que una est de musis.
         Muse enim. i. consonancie dicte sunt a mois quod est
         aqua . . .   (v.13)

       Cf. Giovanni del Virgilio:
         Decima octava de filiabus Acheloi. Per tres filias Acheloi
         intelligimus tres modos quibus omnis melodia perficitur,
         qui sunt vox flatus et tactus. Vox quoad cantum. Flatus
         quoad fistulas. Tactus quoad citharam . . .
           Voce tuba cithara decantat musa triformis
           Hec tres sirenes corda canore trahunt.
         Mater Calliope pater est Achelous amnis . . .   (v.18)

(c) De Plutone et   Est seges alma Ceres, semen Proserpina, tellus
    Proserpina   Pluto, quo sponso sponsa labore parit. (265–6)

(d)   Garrulitatis honus Picarum garula lingua
              Designat fundens iurgia, probra, minas.

                                      (275–6)

       Cf. Giovanni del Virgilio:
         Nona [Musa] vocatur Caliope, que interpretatur optimus
         sonus . . .
           Ergo Caliope docti vox optima cantus
           Picas discordes arguit esse sonus.   (v.22)

VI

(a) De Aragne   Ne quis maiori certet persuadet Aragne
                  Que sub pauperie viscera viva trahit.

De nomine Athenarum	Athanatos grecum sonat immortalis, Athenas Nominat hinc Pallas famaque vivit adhuc.
(b) De Niobe	Proprietas saxi Niobe datur hoc quia durum, Hec quia dura riget firma tenore mali.
(c) De sathiro	Certans cum Phebo satyrus notat insipientis Impar certamen cum sapiente trahi.

(277–84)

Cf. Arnulf:

Niobe regina Latonam spernebat pro duobus filiis suis cum ipsa VII filios et VII filias haberet. Sed a filiis Latone VII filii Niobes et VII filie in simul ocisi sunt. Ipsa in lapidem mutata. Allegoria. Per Niobem habemus superbiam que VII filios habet: pedem, pectus, manum, linguam, nasum, supercilium, oculum, et VII filias, has scilicet: superbum pedis incessum . . . oculi superbiam . . .

(vi.14)

Cf. Giovanni del Virgilio:

Prima transmutatio sexti de Neptuno et Palade debentibus nomen imponere civitati . . . Quapropter nomen imposuit a studio Athenas appellando ab athanatos quod est immortale eo quod sciencia immortalis est. . .   (vi.1)

Vigesima octava est de Niobe conversa in saxum. Per Niobem intelligo superbiam carnis. Sed per ipsam hinc septem filios . . . Sed per septem suas filias . . .   (vi.28)

(d) De Thereo	Historiam tangit describens Terea de quo Musa sophocleo carmine grande canit.

(289–90)

VII

(a) De Arpiis[1]	Tres sunt Arpie, cupidi tria crimina: gliscit Diripit, abscondit; plenior eget inops.
(b) De Medea et Iasone	Auratum vellus Medeam dicimus ipsam, Auro preda fuit hec speciosa magis.
(c)	Virginis est custos draco vel bos, virginis arte Virgine subducta, premia victor habet. Arte tamen magica fieri custodia fertur Quod nequeat valeat aurea lana capi.

(295–302)

(d) De Mirmidoni-bus natis ex formicis	Myrmidonum formica genus sua pignora cauta Esse notat, gentes indicat esse probas.

(313–14)

---

[1] Placed at the end of VI by John of Garland.

VIII

(a) De Minotauro   Taurus adulter erat regisque notarius idem
                    Est dictus pueros progenuisse duos:
                    Hii sunt Mynois, sunt Tauri, sed sapientes
                    Propter adulterium monstra fuisse volunt.
                                                        (321–4)

(b)   The myth of Ariadne is omitted by John of Garland, cf.,
       however, Arnulf, viii.2: Corona Adriagnes in stellas. Quia
       re vera sunt in celo quedam stelle ita in circulo posite ac si
       sint corona. Giovanni del Virgilio, viii.3: Dionisius Bachus
       adinvenit Adrianam et desponsavit eam. Sed quod mutaverit
       eam in signum debes scire quod est quoddam signum stellarum
       in celo simile corone unde et corona dicitur. Quod signum
       Bachus voluit appropriare uxori sue. U. d. e.:

       Suscipiens Bachus stellas de more corone
       Serta mee dixit coniugis esse volo.

(c) De Meleagro   Fax est fatalis Meleagri perdere fortis
                        Rite virum magica qua fuit usa parens.
                    Germanas velat Meleagri pluma vagantes
                        Dum volat instabilis et fugitiva cohors.
    Aliter   Stipes fatalis est frater quo Meleager
                        Occisus mortis tristia fata subit. (327–32)

       Cf. Giovanni del Virgilio:
       Sexta est de morte Meleagri . . . mater interfecit eum
       arte magica. Nam quodam torre accenso fecit artes
       magicas, ut possibile est, et consumpsit eum. U. d. e.:
           Torre puerperii quo sacrum accenderat ignem
           Heu natum magica perdidit arte parens.   (viii.6)

(d) De Fame vex-   Regna tenere Fames lapidosa per arva videtur
     ante Erisictona   Qua se diminuit vir sibi corpus alens.
                                                        (337–8)

IX

(a) De Gerione   Triplex Gerionis caput est in triplice regno
                      Cuius divicie preda fuere viro.
(b) De Caco   Cacus latro fuit et predo tutus in umbra
                      Ignem dic iram sed perit ille tamen.
(c) De Cerbero   Cerberus est mundus, partes illius habentur
                      Tres tria colla canis, vir premit acer eas.
                                                        (357–62)

(d) De thebaica historia   Discuciens Thebas titulos legis historiales
Archanumque tibi fabula nulla tegit.

(389–90)

X

(a) De Mirra   Rem miram mirare novam Mirram per amorem
In mirram verti quam dat amarus amor.

(413–14)

(b) De Adoni   Flos breviter durans iuvenilis dicitur etas
Que cito discedens ut levis umbra fugit.

(419–20)

XI

(a) De serpente volente mordere caput Orphei[1]   Orpheus contemptor mulierum fit muliebris
Preda quibus captus et laceratus obit.
Serpens est livor qui morsu gaudet et umbra,
Ledere cum nequeat ut lapis ille riget.

(b) De Mida   Aurum qui captat Midas designat avarum
Qui ditatus eget fertilitate miser.   (421–6)

Cf. Arnulf:
Mida siquidem rex fuit avarus qui sine auro nichil faciebat . . . (xi.3)

Cf. Giovanni del Virgilio:
Exemplo Mide nobis signatur avarus
Qui cum plus habeat plus eget ipse miser.   (xi.3)

XII

(a) De Lapithis   Dimidiat populos vir equus quoniam domuisse
Frenis hos primo fama recenset equos.

De nuptiis Pyritoi   Piritous duxit uxorem dum caro dum mens,
Dum vicium virtus, mistica bella movent.

(b) De Castore et Polluce et Helena   Iuppiter in cigno Geminos Helenamque creavit.
Iuppiter est virtus ardua, cignus honor.
Ponderis unius gemini nascuntur ab ovo
Partus enim Ledam letus ovare facit.

(445–52)

---

[1] This is the only case of a myth needed to complete the plan of borrowings, and clearly attested in John of Garland, which is not to be found in the extant text of the *Commedia*. Moreover it is obviously one which Dante found attractive, since he chose it to illustrate the conception of poets' allegory in *Convivio*, II.i. Dante may have intended to represent himself under the dual symbol of Orpheus and Hippolytus (visionary and exile), but appears to have subsequently repented in the case of Orpheus, who is now only mentioned in passing in *Inf.* iv.140.

XIII

(a)   Here it is difficult to say how Dante was led to choose the myth which figures in the *Paradiso*: probably he found a marginal gloss drawing attention, in Ulysses' long speech against Ajax (128–381), to the sacrifice of Iphigenia (181–95).

(b) De mutacione   Dic Hecubam latrare canem quia more canino
    Hecube in   Debaccata fuit omnibus orba suis.   (457–8)
    liciscam

> Cf. Arnulf:
> Hecuba in canem dicitur esse mutata quia pre nimio dolore insanuit in sua senectute, sicut faciunt canes. . . .   (xiii.2)

> Cf. Giovanni del Virgilio:
> Secunda est de Hecuba conversa in canem. Hecuba fuit uxor regis Priami, que destructa Troia et interfectis filiis Priami venit ad Polimestorem regem Tracie qui Polidorum Priami et Hecube filium interfecerat. Unde Hecuba effodit sibi lumina. Quapropter lapidata et dilacerata ut canis fuit.
> (xiii.2)

XIV

(a) De Glauco[1]   Est naturalis mutatio gramine facta:
                            Herbe vi Glaucus mergere corpus amat.
                        Antiquis miseris delusio demonum acta
                            Finxit submersos equoris esse deos.
                        In scriptis aliter legi quod scilicet herba
                            Sit Martis mulier nos variare potens.
                                                (469–74)

> Cf. Arnulf:
> Glaucus piscator in mare precipitavit, unde fingitur esse mutatus in deum marinum.   (xiii.8)

> Cf. Giovanni del Virgilio:
> Septima est de Glauco converso in deum marinum . . . comedit de quadam herba que habebat illam proprietatem quod fecit eum submergere se in mare . . . ideo dictum est eum esse conversum in deum maris.   (xiii.7)

---

[1] The divinization of Glaucus occurs at the end of *Met.* XIII and is there treated by Arnulf and Giovanni del Virgilio, but it is transferred to the beginning of XIV by John of Garland.

(b) De Circe   Sic Circe trahit in porcos quos vivere cogit
                      Immunde magica rite nociva viris.
                      Naufragium Scillam Circe facit esse, sed illud
                      Naufragium semper ex meretrice venit.

$$(475-8)$$

Cf. Arnulf:

Circe filia solis dicta quia pulcra fuit, incantationibus suis
socios Ulixis in feras mutavit i. in insensatos nimio amore sui
reddidit . . . Tandem pro amore Ulixis . . . eos ab amore
liberavit . . .

XV

(a)   The choice of the Pheonix as a theme is not determined by the
         texts studied here; Dante must have found it emphasised in
         other marginalia to ll. 391–407 of Ovid's text.

(b) De Ypolito   Ypolitum juvenem mores habuisse seniles
                      Dicimus et carnis exsuperasse malum.

$$(507-8)$$

Cf. Arnulf:

Ipolitus de iuvene in senem quia admodum iuvenis tamen
caste et mature habebat ac si esset senex. Et de mortuo in
vivum quia de fragili in firmum de Ypolito in Virbium i.
in bis virum i. de bruto ad modum ypos i. equi in virtuosum
ac si esset bis vir.   (xv.5)

2

Dante's Imagery

SIR CYRIL HINSHELWOOD

SEVERAL qualities more specific than the general imprint of genius give to Dante's poetry a highly individual and immediately recognizable character. More than perhaps any other poet Dante sees the world with the eye of a painter and he consistently describes it in terms which reflect this habit. The older psychologists distinguished various kinds of imagination, visual, auditory, motor and so on, and whatever the correct form of the psychological analysis may be, there is no doubt that individuals vary very widely in the use they make of different kinds of images in their thinking. It has sometimes been stated that no rational thought is possible except in terms of words. Athletes, artists and people with the power of rapid and decisive action know quite well that this is not true, though the forms of education common at least in Western countries have tended to overemphasize the importance of purely verbal processes. Dante seems to have been a man in whose world the visual image was a form of dominant importance but unlike the painter who uses it directly he translates it into words. The result is discernible throughout the *Divina Commedia*.

Of a certain passage in the *Inferno* a commentator remarked that Dante may well have seen a picture of the incident described: but that Dante might have done just this is precisely the impression given continually, not in isolated passages but everywhere. Indeed no quality of the *Divina Commedia* is more striking than Dante's all-pervading preference for clear, concrete, luminous and colourful visual images, which arouse the feeling that he is not so much describing in the purely literary sense as laying down a specification for a painting, or indeed is engaged in painting before our eyes.

By way of introduction to a rather more systematic examination of this matter it will be useful to mention a few examples. The images in the *Inferno* by which Dante represents times of the day or seasons of the year will serve this purpose. They are limited enough in number to be looked at one after the other, whereby we escape the danger of tendentious selection.

Early morning is referred to thus:

> guardai in alto, e vidi le sue spalle
> vestite già de' raggi del pianeta
> che mena dritto altrui per ogni calle.
> *(Inf.* i.16–18)

> Tempo era dal principio del mattino;
> e il sol montava in su con quelle stelle
> ch'eran con lui, quando l'amor divino
> mosse da prima quelle cose belle;
> *(Inf.* i.37–40)

The first passage simply depicts the shoulder of the hill with the morning sunlight falling on it: the second the posed group of the heavenly bodies. Despite their beauty the descriptions are very matter-of-fact and literal. In the second the group of 'cose belle' created in a certain pattern has now reformed that same pattern before Dante's gaze. Dante's poetic imagination carries him indeed back to the moment of creation, but what he sees there is a group of 'cose belle'. Shakespeare has these intensely visual moments but they are much more fleeting and dissolving than those of Dante.

> what envious clouds
> do lace the severing clouds in yonder east.
> Night's candles are burnt out and jocund day
> stands tiptoe on the misty mountain top.

Most of the content of the Dante passages could have been conveyed by a Botticelli picture, but try and paint the Shakespeare. What trick of the brush could show envy in the streaks of dawn, convey the metaphor of the candles or bring off the idea of expectant day?

In *Inferno*, ii.1 there occurs:

Lo giorno se n'andava, e l'aer bruno
toglieva gli animai che sono in terra
dalle fatiche loro;

(*Inf.* ii.1–3)

which conjures up the picture of the people going home, and
later

Quali i fioretti dal notturno gelo
chinati e chiusi, poi che il sol gl'imbianca,
si drizzan tutti aperti in loro stelo;

(*Inf.* ii.127–9)

which again gives very paintable images.

In the next canto there is the moving and lovely picture
of autumn

Come d'autunno si levan le foglie
l'una appresso dell'altra, infin che il ramo
vede alla terra tutte le sue spoglie:

(*Inf.* iii.112–14)

Here all is ready posed, the tree, an ordered succession
of leaves from branch to ground, and the piled-up heap at
the foot. Dante refers, it is true, to a continuous process but
one easily expressible in terms of instantaneous static
images. Of this translation there are innumerable examples.
It is interesting to contrast the immediate and pictorial
quality of Dante's reference with the restless, retrospective
wandering of Shakespeare's 'bare ruined choirs where late
the sweet birds sang'. Shakespeare himself begins with a
splendid static image, 'when yellow leaves or none or few
do hang . . .' which might almost, though not quite, have
occurred in Dante, but before the painter can get to work
on it it is obliterated by a moving cloud of thoughts,
emotions, regrets and images of a non-visual kind, whereas
even the pathos of Dante's lines receives no more expression
than in the pile of heaped-up leaves at the foot of the tree,
a memorial which he seems to stand and regard in silent
contemplation. The description of the winter scene in
Canto v

E come gli stornei ne portan l'ali,
nel freddo tempo, a schiera larga e piena:

(*Inf.* v.40–41)

also relies for its effect upon form rather than action.

Of all phenomena the passage of time might seem least to lend itself to static representation, yet in Canto VII precisely this is achieved by a simple effect of contrast.

> già ogni stella cade, che saliva
> quando mi mossi,
> > *(Inf.* vii.98–99)

Dante's method is strikingly different from Shakespeare's endless insistence upon the actual processes of change, reflected on and emotionally felt in their whole continuity, as in the sonnet about the three years' duration of his friendship, measured by the cycles of the varying seasons with never a moment of repose.

In Canto XI the time of day is again represented pictorially:

> chè i Pesci guizzan su per l'orizzonta
> e il Carro tutto sovra il Coro giace,
> > *(Inf.* xi.113–14)

strongly contrasting with the metaphorical embroideries of 'night's candles are burnt out'.

At the beginning of Canto XXIV occurs a succession of pictures of early spring where Dante uses a strange and effective way of describing the disappearance of snow. First the peasant looks disconsolately at the landscape:

> lo villanello, a cui la roba manca,
>   si leva e guarda, e vede la campagna
>   biancheggiar tutta, ond' ei si batte l'anca;
> ritorna in casa, e qua e là si lagna,
>   come il tapin che non sa che si faccia.
> > *(Inf.* xxiv.7–11)

Presently the scene changes:

> poi riede e la speranza ringavagna,
>   veggendo il mondo aver cangiata faccia,
>   in poca d'ora, e prende suo vincastro,
>   e fuor le pecorelle a pascer caccia:
> > *(Inf.* xxiv.12–15)

From these passages, and indeed from many others, certain general principles can be gathered. Dante has a

very highly characteristic way of describing actions in terms
of a series of static images, and a preference for conveying
states of mind in terms of the concomitant visual appear-
ances. At one of the most exciting moments in his narrative,
when the demons are advancing on Virgil and himself and
he is in mortal terror for body and soul, he observes:

> E così vid' io già temer li fanti
> ch' uscivan pattegiati di Caprona,
> veggendo si tra nemici cotanti.
> (*Inf.* xxi.94–96)

He refers to his own visual recollection of the soldiers
coming out of the town and of his perceiving their anxiety
at *seeing* themselves surrounded by enemies. Virgil, on
this same occasion, refrains from observing that Dante is
scared, but paints a little picture which is indeed far more
illuminating to the reader than it was likely to be to Dante
(considered as an actor in the drama). Virgil says

> O tu, che siedi
> tra gli scheggion del ponte quatto quatto.
> (*Inf.* xxi.88–89)

All through this exciting action the static pictures abound.
The situation is likened to that observed when a beggar is
set upon by dogs:

> Con quel furor e con quella tempesta,
> ch'escono i cani addosso al poverello,
> che di subito chiede ove s'arresta.
> (*Inf.* xxi.67–69)

Dante keeps asking Virgil: 'Do you see this or that?', as
for example of the Malebranche:

> non vedi tu ch'ei digrignan li denti,
> e colle ciglia ne minaccian duoli?
> (*Inf.* xxi.131–2)

It might well be asked whether these are not simple
devices common to all poets or indeed to all descriptive
writers. But that there is more to it than this becomes
obvious if we do no more than notice the enormous contrast
in the kinds of image used by Dante and by Shakespeare.

There is a complete absence in Dante of all Shakespeare's preoccupation with the insubstantiality and transitoriness of things. Phrases like *such stuff as dreams are made on, all the world's a stage, leave not a wrack behind, last syllable of recorded time, death's dateless night,* are utterly non-visual and completely unpaintable. Dante's material vision would have made little use of them. In Dante no cloud-capped towers would have vanished and left not a wrack behind. They might have fallen like the campanile of St. Mark, forming a splendid heap of rubble over which Dante might have scrambled, with lively depiction of his postures, a scene in which many a painter could have found a congenial subject.

There are various respects in which the appearance of Beatrice to Dante in the Earthly Paradise might be compared, on the one hand, with Oberon's vision of the Vestal and, on the other hand, with the reunion of Hermione and Leontes. But the contrasts in treatment are very great. Dante presents a series of glowing pictures. The eastern sky is rosy, the rest of the heavens fair and clear: the sun is rising behind clouds. Beatrice is there, crowned with olive, robed in flame-colour, mantled in green, and cherubs scatter a cloud of blossoms around her. Dante is profoundly moved, and this too is made visually manifest as he turns to Virgil 'like a small child who runs to his mother when he is frightened or distressed'. The images used by Shakespeare are transient: they are nearer to abstractions and evolve or melt one into another in a way which would elude pictorial pictorial representation. In the Hermione scene there is no moment of contemplative rest, but a ceaselessly shifting tension and play of emotions: nothing pauses.

> The fixture of her eye has motion in't

> Shall I draw the curtain?
> No, not these twenty years

> I'll make the statue move, indeed descend
> And take you by the hand.

> Music, awake her, strike

> Oh, she's warm. . . .

And yet with the theme of this supposedly painted statue glowing with life and colour, it is easy to imagine what a sequence Dante would have made.

Oberon's vision of the mermaid on the dolphin's back promises well from the pictorial point of view, but attention is at once shifted to the effect of her 'dulcet and harmonious breath' on the 'rude sea'; the fair vestal 'throned by the west' is a far from paintable idea, and although 'young Cupid's fiery shaft' may be well enough in this respect its quenching by the 'chaste beams of the watery moon' is intellectual rather than visual.

For Shakespeare indeed the visual almost invariably flees away into the abstract. Not that the visual perception is lacking, but the first brilliant flash of it sets up trains of thought which are pursued into depth after depth. With Dante, on the other hand, the reverse process continually occurs, and the intellectual crystallizes out into the concrete and the visual. Even at the supreme moment of divine revelation at the end of the *Paradiso* he seeks for an instant to embody his apprehension of ultimate truth in a geometrical play of shapes, lights and colours, before he gives up this unequal struggle and draws a veil.

Shakespeare is obsessed with the passage of time and with the uneasy emotions of memory, hope or foreboding. Time for Dante is the position of the sun or of the heavenly bodies. Memory itself becomes translated into terms of immediacy:

> Cominciò egli allor si dolcemente,
> che la dolcezza ancor dentro mi suona.
> (*Purg.* ii.113–14)

It is the present echoing of the melody that here is the reality. Dante would hardly have found much consolation in the thought that his love would endure with the immortality of black ink and indeed such an idea would hardly have formed in his mind at all.

This continual insistence on the immediate and particularly the visual is, more than anything else, what gives to Dante's verse its clear gem-like quality, its richly coloured glow and its sharp light and shade.

In the *Paradiso* his task becomes more difficult than elsewhere, at least as far as the general *mise en scène* is concerned, though the quality of the incidental similes and analogies remains the same as in the rest of the poem. Tremendous play is made with effects of light, but as the late Professor Entwistle once discussed in a paper to the Oxford Dante Society the piling of light on light with ever-increasing intensity is a difficult operation in which success is doubtful. The difficulty is precisely that of an inexperienced painter who, having used his most brilliant tone somewhere in an interior, has nothing left for a sunlit cloud outside.

But if the mounting luminosity of heaven taxes Dante severely, he none the less allows his thoughts to materialize at every turn into what can be clearly visualized. The spirits are wrapped, he says, in their light like silk-worms in their cocoons (and they respond to his approach by glowing more brightly). They are like 'rubies struck by the sun' (*Par.* ix.67) and they give the effect of sunbeams 'striking a sheet of water' (*Par.* ix.112). Even when the heavenly lights have been executing various ballet movements in Canto x they stop and pose in a charming tableau:

> Donne mi parver, non da ballo sciolte,
> ma che s'arrestin tacite ascoltando
> fin che le nuove note hanno ricolte.
> (*Par.* x.79–81)

After yet another ballet movement in Canto x they pose again at the beginning of the next canto

> Poi che ciascuno fu tornato ne lo
> punto del cerchio, in che avanti s'era,
> fermossi come a candelier candelo.
> (*Par.* xi.13–15)

In *Laokoon* Lessing discusses the relations of painting and poetry. He says many acute and profound things about this elusive subject, but some of his principles might have been formulated differently had he drawn fewer examples from Homer and more from Dante, who in some respects offers what comes near to being a refutation of one of the main theses.

Lessing's central theme is roughly that, in principle, poetry describes temporal sequences or actions while painting represents spatial co-existences or objects. But Dante repeatedly does just the opposite of what Lessing prescribes as the function of the poet and follows the canons laid down for the painter. Painting, says Lessing, can only represent a chosen instant of an action and therefore this instant must be the most pregnant one, so as to symbolize that of which the poet would show the whole evolution in time. But Dante does not. Often enough he omits the description of actions altogether and allows what is happening to be inferred from a single vivid picture. The sinners in the water are described:

> che sotto l'acqua ha gente che sospira
> e fanno pullular quest' acqua al summo,
> come l'occhio ti dice, u'che s'aggira.
> (*Inf.* vii.118–20)

As Dante and Virgil approach the city of Dis we are told not of Dante's feelings but of his appearance at a crucial instant:

> Quel color che viltà di fuor mi pinse,
> veggendo il duca mio tornare in volta.
> (*Inf.* ix.1–2)

The most vivid moment of their approach to the city is described in a way perfectly adapted for transfer to canvas. Virgil tells Dante that they are coming to Dis and Dante replies:

> Ed io: 'Maestro, già le sue meschite
> là entro certo nella valle cerno
> vermiglie, come se di fuoco uscite
> fossero.'
> (*Inf.* viii.70–74)

The poet, says Lessing, does not describe objects but relates their effects on people. Dante, on the contrary, conveys the response of people to situations by depicting the expression of their emotions in their outward appearance. His own fear at the gates of Dis is translated into his change of colour. The indignant anger of Flegiàs is described by speaking of him as 'like a man who is hearing of some great deceit which has been practised on him'. In the suicides' wood Dante says that when words and blood came forth from the broken twig he let the branch fall,

> e stetti come l'uom che teme.
>
> (*Inf.* xiii.45)

He could well enough have told us of his own fear but prefers to externalize it and show himself as a figure in a picture. And when later he has been delivering himself of some home truths about Florence, the three whom he has been addressing look at one another 'as men look when they hear the truth':

> Così gridai con la faccia levata;
> e i tre, che ciò inteser per risposta,
> guatar l'un l'altro, come al ver si guata.
>
> (*Inf.* xvi.76–78)

Lessing draws many of his examples from Homer. If Homer wishes to describe Juno's chariot, Lessing points out, he relates the act of its assembly: if he wishes to depict the apparel of a person he enacts the sequence of dressing. This may well be, but nothing like it applies to Dante. He frequently cuts out, almost as though they were not worth describing at all, processes which Homer might well have related at length. Dante indeed takes for granted a not inconsiderable visualizing power in others. He seems to assume, and as the result shows not without justification, that phrases such as 'like a man who has heard bad news' will convey to the reader what it does to him. As the effect of poets like Milton depends in part upon the power of readers to recognize and enjoy literary allusions, so Dante is continually employing what might be called visual allusions. 'Come frati minor vanno per via', he says, and a brilliant memory arises of the little procession in the Italian street, the one figure following behind the other.

There are innumerable examples in the *Commedia* of the description of the internal by means of the external in a way which is by no means forced upon the poet as it would be on the painter. To take a few illustrations from the

Paradiso, Beatrice regards Dante with the look that a mother casts upon a sick child:

> gli occhi drizzò ver me con quel sembiante
> che madre fa sopra figliul deliro.
>
> *(Par.* i.101–2)

Perplexity is depicted by the image of a lamb between two wolves, a dog between two deer:

> Sì si starebbe un agno intra due brame
> di fieri lupi, egualmente temendo;
> sì si starebbe un cane intra due dame.
>
> *(Par.* iv.4–6)

When abashed by the severity of Beatrice Dante does not relate his feelings but describes his attitude:

> Beatrice mi guardò con gli occhi pieni
> di faville d'amor così divini,
> che, vinta, mia virtù diede le reni,
> e quasi mi perdei con gli occhi chini.
>
> *(Par.* iv.139–42)

The souls in Mercury reveal their excitement about Dante's arrival in a picture reminiscent of a Chinese artist who depicts crowds of brilliant fishes flocking to investigate whether something thrown into their pond is good to eat.

> Come in peschiera, ch'è tranquilla e pura,
> traggonsi i pesci a ciò che vien di fuori
> per modo che lo stimin lor pastura;
> sì vid' io ben più di mille splendori
> trarsi ver noi, ed in ciascun s'udia:
> 'Ecco chi crescerà li nostri amori'.
>
> *(Par.* v.100–5)

In *Laokoon* Lessing makes the interesting point that while painters and sculptors appropriately surround mythical figures with objects symbolic of their nature, poets have no need of this device: and indeed that it should be supererogatory for them to employ it. Urania might well be represented in a painting with astronomical instruments in her hand, but such appurtenances would be superfluous in poetry. Lessing distinguishes between the symbolic and the literal and approves the mention by a poet that Vulcan holds a hammer, since this is no mere symbol but a tool of his actual trade relevant to the narrative. This principle is, in fact, sometimes observed by Dante. Urania herself appears and she is unembellished with emblems. Vulcan also occurs with Jove standing by the forge 'in Mongibello alla fucina negra'. But Homer bears a sword when he meets Dante in the first circle:

> 'Mira colui con quella spada in mano,
> che vien dinanzi a'tre sì come sire.'
>
> (*Inf.* iv.86–87)

This is plainly symbolic, but Horace is simply 'satiro' and Ovid merely named. Nevertheless, it goes almost without saying that the whole group of poets form a well-posed piece.

Lessing firmly denies the ability of poets to paint portraits and he quotes various attempts which he adjudges failures. Poets, he says, circumvent the difficulty of describing consecutively what the eye sees as a whole: and they do this by alluding to the effect which beauty or ugliness produce in others, or by speaking of beauty in action, whereby 'Schönheit' is metamorphosed into 'Reiz'. This prescription is in a way the diametrical opposite of Dante's method of revealing emotional effects by the outward signs they produce. Reference has already been made to the scene in the Earthly Paradise just before the unveiling of Beatrice. It is colourful, luminous, and entirely still. But how does Dante cope with the problem of conveying the heavenly beauty which is uncovered before him? Not by Lessing's method. He resorts neither to the subjective nor to the dynamic but presents a dazzling and still static image: 'O isplendor di viva luce eterna', he exclaims, and then quite simply and openly states that nobody could possibly describe it. Without evasion he just declines the challenge.

Unlike most poets Dante usually avoids any metaphor which will not stand up to literal analysis. It is hard to find anywhere in the *Commedia* phrases like 'the viewless wings of Poesy', 'fosterchild of silence', 'injurious distance'. Where others might have referred to 'pale-faced cowardice', Dante speaks of

Quel color che viltà di fuor mi pinse.
                    (*Inf*. ix.1)

No abstractions cloud his references to divine justice, and
he gives just the plain testimony of an eye-witness: 'Dove',
he says, 'si vede di giustizia orribil arte.' Often he is content
simply to illustrate his narrative with a plain parallel from
something he has himself seen. 'Io vidi già' is a formula
used more than once. Instead of seeking metaphorical
epithets to suggest confusion, chaos and disorder, he draws
upon his own memory and says

> Io vidi già cavalier muover campo,
>   e cominciare stormo, e far lor mostra,
>   e talvolta partir per loro scampo.
>   (*Inf*. xxii.1–3)

The opening line of the whole *Commedia* contains, it is
true, the haunting metaphor which has become so famous.
'Nel mezzo del cammin di nostra vita' does not admit of
literal analysis, but in a way it confirms the main thesis
about Dante's imagery. Its development and elaboration
immediately become quite literal and concrete: dark wood,
savage, rough, terrifying: sleepiness, hills, valleys, rays of
the star, the beasts, encounter with Virgil, all these are
untinged with abstraction. There is no talk of vain deluding
joys, sorrow's faded form, or anything of the sort.

The note struck by the opening line itself has, however,
a very important effect of a rather subtle kind. It suggests
the beginning of an allegory and thereby suspends disbelief
at the improbability of an actual visit to the underworld.
The allegorical and the metaphorical very soon fade out,
but the reader has by their temporary aid been translated
unsuspectingly into a world which then becomes so realistic
that he does not stop to think how he came there. This is
one example of a narrative technique which makes the
whole of the *Divine Comedy* seem as authentic and con-
vincing as a true personal experience.

It might perhaps be objected that the various examples
quoted have been unconsciously selected to prove a thesis.
Other poets on occasion use vividly picturesque images:

The blessed Damozel leaned out from the gold bar of Heaven

sounds just what it is, the production of a Pre-Raphaelite painter. But it would be hard to find any poet in whom the pictorial tendency is as marked as it is in Dante. A comparison of the *Inferno* with the sixth book of the *Aeneid* naturally suggests itself, and a cursory look at this may serve to recapitulate the main points which have been raised. Throughout Virgil's account there is a ceaseless, restless movement in contrast with Dante's posed tableaux. There is a mass of detailed and consecutive action in the making of the funeral pyre and in the sacrifices. There is no concentration, as with Dante, on the most pregnant moment of a developing situation, nothing static. The images are seldom clear-cut and indeed they depend for their effect more often upon the sonority of the phrase than upon any visual quality in their evocations:

> Ibant obscuri sola sub nocte per umbram
> perque domos Ditis vacuas et inania regna.
>
> (*Aen.* vi.268–9)

The scenes and situations melt and flow into one another, and Dante's technique of discrete and contrasting images is never employed. Dante's autumn leaves and flocks of birds do indeed appear but they are placed in restless shifting contexts:

> quam multa in silvis autumni frigore primo
> lapsa cadunt folia, aut terram gurgite ab alto
> quam multae glomerantur aves, ubi frigidus annus
> trans pontum fugat et terris immittit apricis.
>
> (*Aen.* vi.309–12)

Virgil is full of abstractions like ultrices Curae, pallentes Morbi and tristis Senectus for which Dante finds little employment. Virgil, too, reels off proper names as though sound meant more to him than concrete imagery, and his landscape is as watery as Dante's is sharply focused. Virgil has to describe on occasion the outward appearance of people, and he is seldom, if ever, content, as Dante so often is, to leave to the external the sole responsibility for revealing the internal, and to allow the facial expression or the attitude to express the thought or the emotions. Aeneas leaves the

Sybil's cavern with sad face and downcast eyes, but the key words of the passage describing this are:

caecosque volutat eventus animo secum.

Dante would have said simply that he stood or walked like a man pondering dark issues.

Whether or not analysis by a computer would confirm the impressions described in this essay, or indeed what kind of information and instructions would be given to the machine to guide its working, is hard to say. The question is perhaps unimportant since the effect produced by Dante on the reader and the emergent quality of what his poetry contains is not determined by frequencies. A more pertinent question is whether these special characteristics of Dante are to any significant extent those of a century, an era, a school or movement or a country. Dante evidently enough belonged to the Middle Ages, but there is no reason to suppose visual imagery played a more prominent role then than before or after, nor does it appear in the least likely that Dante was following a fashion or a rule. His modes of expression seem in the most unforced and natural way to reflect his own mode of thinking, and though people who see and think like painters may conceivably be commoner in Mediterranean lands than in some other parts of the world, I am utterly unable to believe that this special quality of the *Divina Commedia* has any important origin but Dante himself.

3

'Nobilior est vulgaris':
Latin and Vernacular in Dante's Thought

CECIL GRAYSON

THE phrase 'nobilior est vulgaris' in the title of this article puts the finger on a *punctum dolens* of the interpretation of Dante's thought about language. In the sixteenth century the apparent contradiction between *Convivio* and *De Vulgari Eloquentia* in the matter of the nobility of Latin and vernacular seemed to Benedetto Varchi sufficient argument for impugning the authenticity of the latter as a work of Dante.[1] Although this authenticity is no longer in doubt, the contradiction remains and has been variously explained. Recent discussion of Dante's linguistic thought by G. Vinay prompts the present attempt to clarify Dante's views about the vernacular and its relationship to Latin.[2]

At the beginning of *De V.E.*, Bk. I, Dante defines his object and says what he means by *locutio vulgaris*:

... vulgarem locutionem appellamus eam qua infantes assuefiunt ab assistentibus, cum primitus distinguere voces incipiunt; vel, quod brevius dici potest, vulgarem locutionem asserimus, quam sine omni regula nutricem imitantes accipimus. Est et inde alia locutio secundaria nobis, quam Romani gramaticam vocaverunt. Hanc quidem secundariam Greci habent et alii, sed non omnes: ad habitum vero huius

[1] B. Varchi, *L'Ercolano* (con la *Correzione* di L. Castelvetro e la *Varchina* di G. Muzio) (Firenze, 1846), 'Prima dubitazione', pp. 72–73. For Muzio's answer to this and other arguments advanced by Varchi, cf. ibid, pp. 708–14.

[2] G. Vinay, 'Ricerche sul "De Vulgari Eloquentia". I. Lingua "artificiale" "naturale" e letteraria. II. Il "volgare illustre", i "volgari" e gli stili. III. "Apenini devexione clauduntur". IV. "Quod unum fuerit a principio confusionis"'; in *Giorn. Stor. della Lett. Ital.* cxxxvi (1959), fasc. 414, pp. 236–74, and fasc. 415, pp. 367–88. The present article is concerned with Parts I and II of these 'Ricerche'. All references in the article are to the text of *De V.E.* edited by A. Marigo, 3rd ed., with appendix by P. G. Ricci (Florence, 1957).

pauci perveniunt, quia non nisi per spatium temporis et studii assiduitatem regulamur et doctrinamur in illa.

Harum quoque duarum nobilior est vulgaris: tum quia prima fuit humano generi usitata; tum quia totus orbis ipsa perfruitur, licet in diversas prolationes et vocabula sit divisa; tum quia naturalis est nobis, cum illa potius artificialis existat.

Et de hac nobiliori nostra est intentio pertractare.

The distinction made here between the vulgar language and Grammar, between what is natural and original and what constitutes a later 'artificial' creation, is clarified in the chapters which follow. Man alone has a need for speech as a means of communication of his rational faculty. It is in-built in his nature, and to him alone, not to the angels or to the animals, it was conceded by God. Dante does not express the commoner medieval view that this concession was limited to the faculty alone, Adam being left to invent his own language. He states clearly that God gave Adam a complete tongue, that this was Hebrew, and that, if it had not been for the Tower of Babel, we should all be speaking it now. Dante modified this statement in the *Comedy*,[1] but at the time of writing *De V.E.* he believed that the diversity of languages originated with a historical, Biblical event, with a castigation for presumption which overthrew a linguistic unity created and, to his mind at that time, evidently maintained by Grace. Whilst Nimrod got a language to himself (*Inf.* xxxi.67–81), the rest of the participants in the enterprise were smitten according to their occupation at the time of the visitation and were dispersed over the world to form different peoples. This dispersal brought to Europe a threefold idiom situated, according to Dante's geographical indications, in the north, south, and east, and corresponding roughly to what we should call Germanic, Romance, and Byzantine. Dante focuses his attention on the second of these three (for us the western European group), whose language he declares in its turn to be threefold, distinguished by the affirmative particles *oc*, *oïl*, and *sì*. He then argues that these three derive from a common origin on the

[1] *Par.* xxvi.124ff., where Adam states that his original language had disappeared before Babel, and dates the process of inevitable linguistic change from the very beginning.

grounds of common vocabulary: 'Quia multa per eadem vocabula nominare videntur, ut *Deum, celum, amorem, mare, terram, est, vivit, moritur, amat,* alia fere omnia'; and he goes on to exemplify this similarity with brief quotations from Provençal, French and Italian poets. He does not here suggest, however, what precisely their common linguistic origin was.

At this point Dante's concern is with the principle of natural diversity, which had determined not merely the threefold division just referred to, but a multiplicity of variations between the parts and towns of Italy alone, and even within cities themselves. The reason, he explains, lies in the instability and mutability of Man himself, constantly, if unconsciously and imperceptibly, changing his speech just as he alters his habits and dress. With remarkable insight Dante sees the process of natural evolution of language according to time, place, and local conditions, and in relation to human factors of civic life. It is a statement which corresponds very closely to the passage in *Convivio* where he also makes specific reference to *De V.E.*[1] Language varies like customs and dress, 'qui nec natura nec consortio confirmantur, sed humanis beneplacitis localique congruitate nascuntur'. For Dante it is precisely these factors and conditions of change which led to the invention and creation of Grammar:

Hinc moti sunt inventores gramatice facultatis; que quidem gramatica nichil aliud est quam quedam inalterabilis locutionis idemptitas diversis temporibus atque locis. Hec cum de comuni consensu multarum gentium fuerit regulata, nulli singulari arbitrio videtur obnoxia, et per consequens nec variabilis esse potest. Adinvenerunt ergo illam, ne propter variationes sermonis arbitrio singularium fluitantis, vel nullo modo vel saltim imperfecte antiquorum actingeremus autoritates et gesta, sive illorum quos a nobis locorum diversitas facit esse diversos (I. ix.11).

In his notes to this passage Marigo surrounded the text with various explanations which have recently been questioned by Vinay.[2] Marigo would identify the 'inventores

---

[1] The passage is cited below, p. 67.
[2] Marigo, ed. cit., pp. 72–73; Vinay, op. cit., pp. 251ff.

gramatice facultatis' as philosophers, as distinct from grammarians, i.e. the inventors 'di quell' organismo astratto di regole colle quali ogni lingua letteraria è ridotta a sistematica dottrina'. In support of this he cites a thirteenth-century grammarian who states, among other things, that 'omnia ydiomata sunt una gramatica . . . quia nature rerum et modi essendi et intelligendi similes sunt apud omnes . . .'. There is no doubt that this kind of generalization is quite alien to Dante's idea of Grammar as a 'secondary language' confined to Romans, Greeks, and some others. However one may interpret the 'inventores', Grammar is for Dante 'artificialis', a deliberate creation designed to remedy the inconveniences of diversity in the natural languages, and accepted by common consent of many peoples. Latin, 'perpetuo e non corruttibile', was such a creation; but Dante does not tell us precisely when and from what it was created, or what its relationship is to the vernacular. The phrase: 'Est et inde alia locutio secundaria nobis' of I. 1 (*cit. sup.*) suggests perhaps some generic relation, but it is difficult to extract a precise sense of derivation from this, as Dante is speaking in general terms about vernacular and Grammar.

Marigo's interpretation of Dante's view of this relationship is stated in his Introduction (p. lxii):

Essi [i.e. the 'inventors' of grammar] hanno così aperto la via ai compilatori di speciali grammatiche, i quali hanno ridotto a regola e stabilità, nei vocaboli, nelle forme e nei costrutti, alcune lingue letterarie come il latino ed il greco, naturalmente fondandosi sull' *auctoritas* dei più eccellenti poeti e prosatori greci e latini, talora risalendo da essi anche alla lingua naturale del popolo.

To which he later adds (p. lxiv):

Egli [i.e. Dante] sa che questa naturale mobilità aveva avuto anche 'lo latino romano' nei secoli gloriosi dei suoi grandi poeti, storici ed oratori, sull 'uso dei quali si potè compilare nel tempo della sua decadenza letteraria, la grammatica, che lo rese perpetuo e non corruttibile, come in quei secoli gloriosi Dante pensa fosse già avvenuto per la greca;

and Marigo here refers to *Conv.* 1. xi.14. Could this in fact have been the way in which Dante saw the situation? It may be questioned in the first place whether Dante was aware of any variations in 'lo latino romano' when quoting Cicero in *Conv.* I.xi.14. Here, criticizing those who oppose the Italian vernacular 'per una maliziata scusa', and blame the instrument when they should blame their own lack of skill, Dante adds:

Contra questi cotali grida Tullio nel principio d'un suo libro che si chiama Libro di Fine de' Beni, però che al suo tempo biasimavano lo latino romano e commendavano la grammatica greca per simiglianti cagioni che questi fanno vile lo parlare italico e prezioso quello di Provenza.

The text of Cicero which Dante had in mind contains no reference to the 'mobilità del latino', but simply to a prejudice against transferring into Latin (*latinis litteris*) what philosophers had treated with consummate doctrine in Greek (*graeco sermone*).[1] It was a question of what seemed to some appropriate and fixed by tradition; and this is a parallel in Dante's mind to the case of Italian and Provençal. If he had really understood it as an opposition between a changeable Latin and a fixed Greek, the parallel would have been inappropriate ('simiglianti cagioni'?); and furthermore, such a view would have been far more suitably used (and Dante never uses it) to support the possible claims of a changeable Italian against a fixed Latin. I would maintain, therefore, that in this passage of *Convivio* Dante simply means Latin *versus* Greek without any implications of change.

Though Dante clearly says of Grammar, in the passage quoted above from *De V.E.*, that it is 'invariable', Marigo (p. 73) glosses the phrase 'nec variabilis esse potest': 'per le forme non per i vocaboli. Che anche una lingua "artificiale" si muti attraverso i secoli rinnovando i vocaboli, Dante lo sa, oltre che dalle differenze che notava tra il latino classico e medievale, anche da Orazio . . .', and he refers to *Conv.* II.xiii.10, where Dante cites *Ars Poetica*, 70ff. This statement is at variance with the passage from his Introduction (*cit. sup.*) where Marigo had written that

---

[1] Cf. *Il Convivio*, ed. Busnelli and Vandelli (Florence, 2nd ed., 1954), vol. i, p. 72 and notes 10, 12; also Vinay, p. 244.

Grammar also fixed 'vocaboli'; but it also raises further
questions about Dante's conception of Latin and Grammar
which need clarification, especially as the passage in *Conv.*
II.xiii involves far more than 'vocaboli'. Here Dante likens
the Moon to Grammar on account of two properties:

> . . . l'una si è l'ombra che è in essa, la quale non è altro che raritade
> del suo corpo, a la quale non possono terminare li raggi del sole e
> ripercuotersi così come ne l'altre parti; l'altra si è la variazione de la
> sua luminositade, che ora luce da uno lato e ora luce da un altro,
> secondo che lo sole la vede. E queste due proprietadi hae la Gramatica:
> chè, per la sua infinitade, li raggi de la ragione in essa non si terminano,
> in parte spezialmente de li vocaboli; e luce or di qua or di là in tanto
> quanto certi vocabuli, certe declinazioni, certe construzioni sono in
> uso che già non furono, e molte già furono che ancor saranno: sì come
> dice Orazio nel principio de la Poetria quando dice: 'Molti vocabuli
> rinasceranno che già caddero.'

I have found no satisfactory commentary on the meaning
of this passage.[1] In the general context of the identification
of the various heavens with the sciences, I take it that Dante
refers here to Grammar as 'scientia linguae' in its broadest
sense. If so, whilst it would embrace all 'fixed' language, it
reflects imperfectly the rays of reason[2]; and according as
it stands to these rays, so some parts of Grammar (words,
constructions, declensions) are illuminated, while others go
into shadow. That is, Grammar (=Moon) has a fixed con-
stitution, whose parts come and go, as it were, with time and
usage. The passage from Horace refers explicitly to usage:

> Multa renascentur, quae iam cecidere; cadentque
> Quae nunc sunt in honore vocabula, si volet usus,
> Quem penes arbitrium est et jus et norma loquendi.

[1] The commentary of Busnelli and Vandelli (ed. cit., pp. 194–6) is of
little or no assistance for interpreting the comparison. Vinay does not discuss
the passage.

[2] I am assuming that the 'imperfection' lies with 'reason' rather than with
Grammar, though the 'infinity' of the latter, represented by its 'shadows'
(*raritade*), which constitute an inability of the Moon to reflect, not of the
'reason' to shine, suggest possibly the opposite. It seems feasible to deduce
from this that perhaps Grammar does not contain all expression? I can only
pose the question, and suggest a possible interpretation of this puzzling
comparison, which is of considerable importance for understanding Dante's
view of change in Grammar through usage.

If Dante really understood this to apply to Latin, it is
difficult to reconcile it with his earlier statements in *Conv.*
I, where in the same paragraph he declares Latin 'perpetuo
e non corruttibile', and speaks of changes in 'vocabuli', not in
Latin, but in the vernacular ('vedemo ne le cittadi d'Italia . . .
da cinquanta anni in qua molti vocaboli essere spenti e nati e
variati'), and with his statement that 'lo volgare seguita
uso, e lo latino arte'. He would here be admitting (in *Conv.*
II.xiii) that 'lo latino seguita uso', at least to the extent that
within the ordained limits of Grammar elements disappear
and reappear according to usage; their perpetuity and
incorruptibility remaining unaffected by this kind of cyclic
change. This reconciliation of Dante's statements involves
accepting two different views of 'uso'—one which corrupts
the vernacular, and one which does not corrupt, but simply
periodically selects from Grammar.

In order to take this point farther, we may turn to another
major aspect on which Vinay questions Marigo's interpretation, viz., that Dante realized Grammar to be a
codification of a literary language based on the *auctores*.
First of all, it seems clear that Dante held a view about
'grammatica' = Latin, quite opposite to that which we know
to be true. Whereas we see the Romance languages of *oc*,
oïl, and *sì* as descendants of the Latin language spread over
Europe by Roman conquest, Dante sees Grammar as a
deliberate creation effected by common agreement at a
point in time when the *idioma trypharium* was nearer than
in his own day to its common origin, whatever that may
have been. At no time does he imply that 'grammatica' was
identified with a particular spoken tongue, though it may be
inferred from his writings that Grammar bore some physical
relation to the variety of languages whose differences its
stability was intended to remedy. The questions discussed
above are relevant to this relationship. There is no certain
evidence that Dante made a distinction between 'lo latino
romano' and Grammar. If this were implied in *Conv.* I.xi he
must have believed that Cicero wrote in a pre-grammatical
vernacular ('latino romano') as opposed to 'la grammatica greca'. What then of Horace and the passage
quoted above from *Ars Poetica*? Was this for Dante written

in 'latino romano' (not 'grammatica'), and was Horace
speaking about changes through usage of a vernacular? If
so, this could hardly be evidence for Dante about variations
in a 'lingua artificialis'. But these hypotheses do not correspond to Dante's consistent allusions to such writers and
their idiom; all of which suggest that Dante believed they
wrote in the established and stabilized medium he calls
'grammatica'. As Vinay puts it, 'Virgilio ... è un poeta che,
come tutti gli altri "regulares", parte da un "sermo" e da
un' "ars" già dati: non è fonte di grammatica ma l'adopera'.[1]

Where then did Dante think Grammar came from? He
gives no indication that he believed it of literary formation
or that he knew it belonged to the period of 'decadenza
letteraria' and after. It was 'invented' and accepted 'by
common consent of many peoples'. Had he thought it a
literary creation, the result of a tradition of 'doctores
illustres', he might have found there a basis for a theory of
the 'vulgare illustre'. But at no time does he hint at such an
origin, or exploit any such similarity of historical pattern.
It would have been difficult in any case for him to do so, for
it would have struck at the very roots of his opposition
between the vernacular as 'natural' and Grammar as
'artificial'—unless one assumes he was aiming in *De V.E.*
at a similar *grammatical* regularization of the vernacular.
But this is, I believe, an untenable assumption, despite
Dante's desire to achieve a relatively greater 'stabilitade' of
vernacular eloquence. In his intentions with regard to the
vernacular Dante is clearly the poet and not a grammarian.

Some clues as to the sources of Grammar, and therefore
of its relationship to the vernacular, are given by Dante in
De V.E. I.x, where he discusses the relative merits and claims
to pre-eminence of the languages of *oc, oïl*, and *sì*. Hesitating
which to prefer, he finds some element of distinction
'... eo quo gramatice positores inveniuntur accepisse *sic* adver-
bium affirmandi: quod quandam anterioritatem erogare
videtur Ytalis, qui *si* dicunt', i.e. in the fact that the creators of
Grammar took *sic* as the affirmative particle, thereby apparently conferring some precedence on the Italians who use *sì*.

[1] Vinay, p. 251.

He further finds that whilst French may claim pre-eminence for achievement in prose, and Provençal for priority in verse, Italian has two merits in its favour: 'primo quidem quod qui dulcius subtiliusque poetati vulgariter sunt, hii familiares et domestici sui sunt, puta Cynus Pistoriensis et amicus eius; secundo quia magis videtur inniti gramatice que comunis est, quod rationabiliter inspicientibus videtur gravissimum argumentum': i.e. firstly because the 'sweeter' and 'subtler' poets, Cino and Dante, have used it, and secondly because it is seen to rest more on grammar (a most important argument). At first sight these passages may seem to constitute two contradictory statements within fifteen lines of each other. Marigo attenuates the effect of the earlier passage by glossing: 'se infatti il suo avverbio asseverativo corrisponde per forma e significato al *sic* della lingua latina, questo è segno che il volgare italiano ha con questa una più schietta conformità che gli altri due dell' '*Ydioma tripharium* . . .'; to the later passage he adds a note which concludes by speaking of 'una comunanza che ha le sue radici nelle lingue parlate d'*oc*, *oïl*, e in modo particolare in quella di *sì*, la quale mostra più chiara e più integra che nelle altre due lingue l'impronta della sua discendenza storica dalla lingua di Roma'.[1]

It will appear doubtful from what has been argued so far that this can be the proper explanation of Dante's text. Zingarelli was nearer the truth when he wrote in relation to the first passage: 'vedendo che il nostro *sì* è una stessa parola con la particella affermativa della grammatica, ovvero latino, *sic*, Dante ne argomentava che la nostra si accostasse di più alla nobile forma anteriore, perché i dotti dovevano aver prescelto le più nobili parole.'[2] This is substantially the explanation developed by Vinay and applied also to interpret the second passage. On the face of things, it seems completely contradictory that Dante should mean by this second passage that Italian, a natural and so more noble language, should gain merit by resting more on Latin, which is artificial—unless we qualify it by superimposing, as Vinay does, the sense of the first passage, viz. that by 'resting more on Latin' Italian demonstrates its greater proximity to its origins. But it is strange that Dante should have thought it necessary to make this point twice in the same chapter, clearly the first time, and obscurely (at least for us) the second, insisting that it is 'gravissimum argumentum'. This fact in itself is sufficient to suggest that a different interpretation must be given to one or the other, preferably the second. The context of the first passage is linguistic, that of the second explicitly literary. It would seem odd that Dante should introduce into an argument which compares French prose, Provençal verse, and Italian poetry, a final thrust of a purely linguistic character (which if we are correct, he had already made anyway in another form). We should logically expect a further literary qualification. It is worth recalling that *videtur* is missing from the Berlin MS in the important phrase: 'magis *videtur* inniti gramatice que comunis est'; and that the other two authoritative MSS, Grenoble and Trivulziano, both read *videntur*. *Videtur* is a critical emendation proposed by Rajna and subsequently accepted by all editors and critics.[1] The plural would make Cino and Dante the subject, not Italian. In the interpretation of this difficult passage, the possibility cannot be lightly rejected that Dante understood as a merit of literary Italian the fact that he and Cino, more than the writers of French prose or Provençal verse, 'rested on Grammar', in the sense that Grammar was a language of art. Whatever Dante may say about the greater nobility of the natural vernacular in *De V.E.*, he leaves no doubt that he regarded the artistic achievement of Latin as superior and as a model of imitation. Indeed a 'resting on Grammar', in the sense of literary imitation, will be advocated by him in

---

[1] *Il trattato De Vulgari Eloquentia*, per cura di P. Rajna (Florence, 1896) p. 51 (Grenoble and Trivulziano MSS); *Dantis Alagherii De V. E., libri II*, recensuit L. Bertalot (Frankfurt, 1917) (Berlin MS). All discussion of the passage seems to have moved from Rajna's integration, starting from F. D'Ovidio, 'Sul trattato *De V.E.* di Dante Alighieri', in *Versificazione italiana e arte poetica medievale* (Milan, 1910), especially pp. 499–500, down to A. Schiaffini, *Lettura del De V.E.* (Rome, 1960), especially pp. 116ff., and A. Pagliaro, 'I primissimi signa e la dottrina linguistica di Dante', in *Nuovi saggi di critica semantica* (Rome, 1956), pp. 213–39.

De V.E. II. iv and vi; and he later claimed to have taken his 'bello stile' from Virgil. But, whether we read *videntur* or *videtur*, it seems necessary to seek some literary interpretation of the important phrase rather than to impose, with no little difficulty, a linguistic explanation.

My suggestion, therefore, is that the first passage indicates a linguistic affinity between Italian and Latin, the second a degree of stylistic assimilation. If Dante had wished the second to say the same as the first, it would have been more logical for him to have written: 'quia magis ei videtur inniti gramatica', i.e. that grammar leans more on the Italian vernacular. It seems probable that he wished to make quite a different point in stricter relation to the literary experience of the vernacular. Nor is 'que comunis est' a real obstacle; as Vinay rightly observes, this does not necessarily mean 'which is closely related linguistically to the languages of *oc*, *oïl*, and *sì*', but simply, 'which is common to many peoples'. If we do take the passage in the limited sense of linguistic similarity to Latin, we come up against a further apparent difficulty, that of Sardinian. In his review of the different languages of Italy in *De V.E.* I, Dante writes: 'Sardos etiam, qui non Latii sunt, sed Latiis associandi videntur, eiciamus, quoniam soli sine proprio vulgari esse videntur, gramaticam, tanquam simie homines imitantes: nam *dominus nova* et *domus novus* locuntur' (I. xi.7). From this clearly contemptuous passage it is evident that Dante saw Sardinians 'resting on Grammar' in a totally different sense. Having no natural vernacular, they use an artificial language and use it badly. Dante may have got his Sardinian wrong, but his point is unmistakable: a corrupted artificial substitute for a natural language is despicable. It is certainly not comparable with any measure of linguistic or stylistic assimilation of Latin by peoples who possess a vernacular of their own, which is in some way related to it.

Proceeding from discussion of *De V.E.* I.x, we may deduce that Dante believed Grammar to have been created by unnamed 'inventors' from the multiplicity of vernacular usages by some process of selection, among which the fact that they chose the affirmative particle *sic* indicates a preference for the vernacular of Italy. In other words, any pre-eminence does not derive from the fact that the Italian vernacular is like Latin, but from the fact that the grammarians in some measure chose to make Latin like the vernacular of Italy. This serves to eliminate still further any possible contradiction between Sardinian, which apes Latin, and Italian, which has quite a different affinity with Latin. But how far did he believe this affinity extended? His statement at the beginning of *De V.E.* I, that grammar can be attained only by a few and with considerable labour, suggests no close relation. Certain parts of *Conv.* I seem to place an unbridgeable abyss between them. In I.vi, he uses as an argument to explain his writing a vernacular commentary on his *canzoni* the fact that Latin would not have had knowledge and understanding of them:

Lo latino conosce lo volgare in genere, ma non distinto: ché se esso lo conoscesse distinto, tutti li volgari conoscerebbe, perché non è ragione che l'uno più che l'altro conoscesse; e così in qualunque uomo fosse tutto l'abito del latino, sarebbe l'abito di conoscenza distinto de lo volgare. Ma questo non è; ché uno abituato di latino non distingue, s'elli è d'Italia, lo volgare inghilese da lo tedesco; né lo tedesco, lo volgare italico dal provenzale. Onde è manifesto che lo latino non è conoscente de lo volgare.

He did not believe, at least at the moment of writing this paragraph, that any close relation of intercommunicability existed between Latin and any vernacular or with one more than another. It appears that he had gone some way to modifying this view in *De V.E.* by establishing some kind of linguistic connexion between Latin and vernacular, and with Italian more than others. To credit Dante, however, with more than the most schematic idea of the history of this connexion is to attribute to him a knowledge he probably did not possess, or at least to risk inserting into his thought problems which he did not even pose to himself at all.[1]

[1] If he did have such knowledge and posed these relationships to himself clearly, Dante was an exception and well ahead of his times. The view was persistent well into the fifteenth century that Latin was 'una invenzione scolastica più tosto intesa che saputa da' molti', separated by a wide margin from the vernacular of Rome (L. B. Alberti, preface to *Famiglia*, Bk. III;

With these remarks before us on Dante's thought about Latin and vernacular, we are in a position to sketch the progress of his views from his early work down to *De V.E.* In chap xxv of *Vita Nuova* he digresses on the history of vernacular poetry in order to defend his own use of prosopopoeia, and draws a parallel between ancient poetic tradition in Latin and the relatively recent tradition of vernacular poetry born of the need to communicate with woman, 'a la quale era malagevole d'intendere li versi latini'. His discussion is on the plane of poetic composition and licence, justifying the legitimacy of certain procedures in the modern by their presence in the older tradition. He sees no relationship between them except of greater or lesser antiquity and reputation, and presents Latin and vernacular as two separate, static entities, without reference to any linguistic affinity or dependence, and without any reference to change. He is exclusively concerned with the practical origin of vernacular poetry, with a question of usage, with circumstances which at a point not very distant in time dictated the necessity to diverge from the tradition of the 'literati poete', and which consequently determined the narrow artistic field of operation of the vernacular, that of love poetry. The motive for this concern is clearly that of a polemic from the standpoint of the *stilnovo*, against Guittone and the 'alquanti grossi' who exceeded those limits and were thought to be good poets because they were the first. At the same time, in placing vernacular poetry on the same plane as Latin 'secondo alcuna proporzione', he takes the first step towards the principle of stylistic imitation of the Latin poets he will enunciate more clearly in *De V.E.*

Some ten years later, when writing *Convivio*, his ideas and attitude about the range and capabilities of the vernacular had obviously changed. The narrow practical origins of vernacular poetry have been left behind, and the polemic against the pre-stilnovo poets of the Italian tradition has given place to a vigorous affirmation of Italian in

Flavio Biondo, *De locutione romana;* cf. C. Grayson, *A Renaissance controversy: Latin or Italian,* Oxford, 1960). This fact ought to make us cautious in reading into Dante's thought knowledge and historical interpretations which only evolved much later.

competition with other contemporary languages, especially Provençal, and in rivalry with Latin—not the Latin of poets of the past, but the Latin of the modern schoolmen. His comment on Latin in *Conv.* I is compounded of defence and attack, so that, while on the one hand he declares Latin superior, on the other he demonstrates its relative inferiority for his present purposes. His first argument for writing his commentary in Italian is that Latin would not have served with due obedience his Italian *canzoni*:

Ché, primamente non era subietto ma sovrano, e per nobiltà e per vertù e per bellezza. Per nobiltà, perché lo latino è perpetuo e non corruttibile. Onde vedemo ne le scritture antiche de le comedie e tragedie latine, che non si possono transmutare, quello medesimo che oggi avemo; che non avviene del volgare, lo quale a piacimento artificiato si transmuta. Onde vedemo ne le cittadi d'Italia, se bene volemo agguardare, da cinquanta anni in qua molti vocabuli essere spenti e nati e variati; onde se 'l picciol tempo così transmuta, molto tempo transmuta lo maggiore. Sì ch'io dico, che se coloro che partirono d'esta vita già sono mille anni tornassero a le loro cittadi, crederebbero la loro cittade essere occupata da gente strana, per la lingua da loro discordante. Di questo si parlerà altrove più compiutamente in uno libello ch'io intendo di fare, Dio concedente, di Volgare Eloquenza. (I.v.7–10).

There is no need to doubt this statement as a promise for the future, if for a future little removed in time. The view expressed of Latin as more noble than the vernacular because of its static incorruptibility is one of a language virtually without a history. The Latin of ancient writers is 'quello medesimo che noi avemo'. Outside this particular quality, whatever else Dante says in *Conv.* I about Latin and vernacular he gives with one hand and takes away with the other: only this point of greater nobility remains firm on the basis of the contrast between stability and mobility. Whilst he goes on to explain the greater 'vertù' of Latin ('lo latino molte cose manifesta concepute ne la mente che lo volgare fare non può'), and also its greater 'bellezza' ('quello sermone è più bello ne lo quale più debitamente si rispondono le parole; e più debitamente si rispondono in latino che in volgare, però che lo volgare seguita uso, e lo latino arte'), nevertheless he concludes his impassioned apology for the vernacular by claiming precisely these two qualities of 'vertù' and 'bellezza' for his commentary:

> Chè per questo comento la gran bontade del volgare di sì si vedrà; però che si vedrà la sua *vertù*, sì com'è per esso altissimi e novissimi concetti convenevolmente, sufficientemente e acconciamente, *quasi come per esso latino,* manifestare . . .
>
> . . . questo comento, nel quale si vedrà l'agevolezza de le sue sillabe, le proprietadi de le sue costruzioni e le soavi orazioni che di lui si fanno; le quali chi bene agguarderà, vedrà essere piene di dolcissima e d'amabilissima *bellezza* (I.x.12).

It might be claimed that Dante has here overcome the lesser nobility of the vernacular in spirit; but in the letter of *Conv.* I, where the qualities of 'nobiltà', 'vertù', and 'bellezza' are separately dealt with, he quite clearly has not. The so-called contradiction with the beginning of *De V.E.* remains to be resolved, and it should be seen in the terms in which Dante sees. The condition of 'nobiltà' is seen in *Conv.* I as stability. The capacities to express ideas (vertù), and to do so with appropriate and adequate terms (bellezza), are other qualities: they are not the specific qualifications of nobility. In discussion of this problem, these have been and still are more often than not confused.

For Rajna the contradiction was non-existent, 'giacché il volgare del *Convivio* e quello di cui qui [in *De V.E.*] si parla, sono cose ben distinte; il primo è specificatamente il Volgare nostro; il secondo è la favella in universale, in quanto sia, in modo spontaneo, di tutti gli uomini, dovunque e in ogni tempo, e s'identifica quindi colla facoltà stessa del linguaggio'.[1] As Nardi and others have observed, Dante could not and does not conceive the vernacular in the abstract, and the general treatment in *De V.E.* must include 'il volgare nostro', which is in effect the main object and subject of the work.[2] The contradiction is, therefore, not resolvable in this way. Parodi's view, subscribed to also by

[1] Quoted by A. Schiaffini, op. cit., p. 61, together with the opinion of Nardi, without, however, making clear his own.
[2] B. Nardi, 'Il linguaggio', in *Dante e la cultura medievale* (Rome, 1942), p. 161.

Busnelli and Vandelli in their edition of *Convivio*, is as follows:

... nelle due opere il Poeta parla secondo due diversi punti di vista, i quali sono entrambi, al loro posto, ragionevoli. Se si guarda bene, la contradizione non riguarda tanto la relazione tra volgare e latino, quanto quella tra natura ed arte; ma è certo che, in un dato senso, la natura è più nobile dell'arte, e quindi il volgare,—che per il *De V.E.* è il linguaggio naturale e universale,—è più nobile dell 'artificiata grammatica; in un altro senso, è più nobile l'arte in quanto è un ulteriore progresso della natura.[1]

It is difficult to accept this explanation of the 'contradiction'. Dante never says in *Convivio* that Latin is more noble because it follows art, but simply because it is fixed and incorruptible (it is more *beautiful* because it follows art). What he does say in *Convivio*, and he repeats it in *De V.E.*, is that Latin is artistically superior ('sovrano per vertù e per bellezza'), and at the same time for this very reason he wishes to rival or assimilate some of its qualities in the vernacular. Therefore, on a strict interpretation of the letter of these two works, the sole basic difference and contradiction is in terms of 'nobiltà', and this rests on the quality of immutability, and on nothing else. On this ground it appears to me that there is a complete *volte-face* between *Convivio* and *De V.E.* on this particular point, and its importance can only be obscured and diminished by talking in terms of two different points of view which bring in issues of art, where Dante did not put them. Though he does not mention nobility at this point, the issue is not clearly stated in Nardi's neat contrapuntal summing-up: 'Lo svolgimento del pensiero di Dante è dunque evidentissimo. Prima aveva detto che "il volgare seguita uso e lo latino arte"; ora, invece, che il volgare seguita la natura, e la grammatica l'artificio e la convenzione.'[2] The terms are not opposed in this fashion by Dante: the first is a comparison on the plane of art, and is as valid in *De V.E.* as it was in *Convivio*, though the purpose of *De V.E.* is to remedy this shortcoming of the vernacular; the second is a comparison on a

[1] *Convivio*, ed. cit., Appendici (to Bk. I), 'Nobiltà del volgare e del Latino', pp. 87–89.
[2] Op. cit., p. 163.

linguistic plane, and is the fundamental justification of a theoretical kind for the whole treatment of vernacular eloquence. It is the latter which I am concerned to separate more rigorously than hitherto from considerations which do not enter into Dante's presentation of the matter of greater or lesser nobility of Latin and vernacular.

In *Conv.* I there is considerable emotional fervour for the vernacular and great respect for Latin; but there is no relation between them of a historical or human kind: they are not intercommunicable. At this point the greater nobility of Latin rests with its stability. Its superiority in other respects Dante recognizes, but already here challenges with his Italian commentary. In *De V.E.* I his thought embraces all vernaculars including Italian, and he has found a new equation between nobility and nature. He has discovered a historical perspective which might be seen as the reverse, on a linguistic plane, of the literary one he sketched in *Vita Nuova* xxv. In *De V.E.* the greater antiquity belongs to the vernaculars, inherent in Man's nature, and evolving with the many changes in his needs in time and space. Against this background Latin = Grammar appears as an artificial creation of men to meet a practical necessity, related in some way to the vernaculars but, unlike them, fixed and unchanging. It is 'locutio secundaria', and as such has second place behind the first and more noble language, the vernacular. Dante has shifted his ground about nobility in the matter of language, and whatever else he may later say or do about Latin, he does not alter this qualification.

The seeds of this change are already apparent in *Convivio* itself. In Bk. I he makes references to nobility, which point in the direction of *De V.E.* Polemicizing against those who have debased Latin, he proclaims the greater utility of his vernacular as 'datore d'utile dono':

Lo dono veramente di questo comento è la sentenza de le canzoni a le quali fatto è, la qual massimamente intende inducere li uomini a scienza e a vertù . . . Questa sentenza non possono non avere in uso quelli ne li quali vera nobiltà è seminata per lo modo che si dirà nel quarto trattato; e questi sono quasi tutti volgari . . . (I.ix.7–8).

There is here the promise of an equation between true nobility and the vernacular which will find confirmation in

Bk. IV. There is also an interesting association in Bk. I between 'bontà', nobility and vernacular, for he finds 'bontà de l'animo' in 'principi, baroni, cavalieri e molt' altra nobile gente, non solamente maschi ma femmine, che sono molti e molte in questa lingua, volgari e non litterati' (I. ix. 5). And when we turn to Bk. IV the equation seems completed with the addition of Nature when Dante speaks of 'l'umana bontade in quanto in noi è da la natura seminata e che nobilitade chiamare si dee' (IV. iv. 1). The whole question of the vernacular in *Convivio* is bound up with moral problems of goodness, nobility, nature, in such a way as to leave almost cold and isolated the incorruptibility (= nobility) of Latin.

Vinay has argued that Dante's conception of nobility in *Conv.* IV undergoes a radical change, and that this has bearing on the relationship of Latin to Italian.[1] The question merits investigation. Dante makes the equation (*cit.* above) between 'umana bontade' and nobility in IV. iv. 1; but as he proceeds he gives further qualifications on nobility, especially in ch. xvi:

. . . se volemo riguardo avere de la comune consuetudine di parlare, per questo vocabulo 'nobilitade' s'intende perfezione di propria natura in ciascuna cosa.

. . . così manifestamente vedere si può che generalmente questo vocabulo, cioè nobilitade, dice in tutte cose perfezione di loro natura.

But before we jump to conclusions and ask ourselves (with Vinay) whether Dante therefore thought Latin perfect in *Conv.* I, because he says it is more noble than the vernacular, or the vernacular perfect in *De V.E.*, because he says it is more noble than Grammar, we should underline strongly the phrase *di propria natura* and not ask nobility to be an absolute. Furthermore, these are what Dante calls generally accepted definitions, which he uses as a starting-point for a disquisition on 'la nobilitade umana', and this he again equates with 'umana bontade' (xxi. 1), with virtue which is both innate and perfectible. The demonstration and cultivation of this is a prime object of the whole of *Convivio*. I cannot follow Vinay, therefore, when he argues that:

[1] Vinay, pp. 255–8.

. . il rapporto natura-nobiltà è prospettato nel quarto del *Convivio* in tutt 'altro modo: 'nobilior' perché naturale il volgare del *De V.E.*, 'nobilior' qui ciò che è più perfetto secondo la propria natura [and here he cites the second definition from ch. xvi, cit. sup.] . . . Prova sperimentale di nobiltà i 'frutti' [and he cites: 'per lo cammino diritto è da vedere, questa diffinizione che cercando vae, per li frutti' of iv.xvi.10] . . . Orbene, non è il latino perfetto nella sua natura di strumento di comunicazione tra le 'gentes' dell 'orbe imperiale o cristiano? Non sono perfetti i suoi frutti che si chiamano *Eneide* o *Farsalia?* È tutto intero il sistema del *De V.E.* che crolla. . . .

In the first place it must be made clear that it is Vinay and not Dante who is applying these criteria of nobility *to language* at this point, and with a rigidity entirely his own. Dante never on any occasion said that either Latin or vernacular were noble or not noble *tout court*. On separate occasions he said that one was more noble than the other. It is totally unjustifiable to argue that because nobility is perfection 'di propria natura' (and this is what Dante says is a generally accepted definition; it is not his own of human nobility), therefore, as Latin and its literary monuments are perfect (which Dante does not in fact say), Latin is by implication more noble than Italian. It is quite another matter to recognize a change in Dante's historical and political outlook about Rome in *Conv.* iv, but does it necessarily follow that his view of Latin must have changed? Vinay thinks so: 'Di fronte alla provvidenzialità dell 'Impero, alla "santità" di un popolo cui Dio non ha posto "termine di cose né di tempo", lo stesso criterio di "artificialità" e di "naturalità", addotto per difendere il volgare, perde ogni forza di persuasione . . .' and he argues from this the greater nobility of Latin, as we have seen above, resulting in the collapse of the edifice of the *De V.E.*:

. . . resta il volgare illustre, ma come l'Italia di fronte al mondo. E il latino? Dante non gli opporrà mai più il volgare. Scriverà la Commedia in volgare perché in lui prevarrà, come è sempre prevalsa, l'umanità del poeta sulla coerenza del pensatore, ma chi scrisse che pensò di scriverla in latino non ha avuto torto, almeno nel senso che c'era qualche buona ragione per farglielo pensare.

The conclusion appears excessive. At no point in *Conv.* iv or in *De Monarchia* does Dante mention Latin as a language or identify it exclusively with the Romans. His confidence in the vernacular seems at no point impaired. We have no evidence that he had changed his mind about Latin as an 'artificial' creation, or that he necessarily must have identified its universality with the providential universal empire of the Romans. If he ever did ask himself whether he was right in thinking that Virgil had written in an 'artificial' language, the reflection might have given more weight to Dante's writing the *Comedy* in his own vernacular rather than to his writing it in Virgil's. The *Comedy* contains ample evidence that Dante had not abandoned his idea of natural linguistic change, and of the inevitability of a process of making and superseding reputations in art.[1] Vinay maintains that the 'reductio ad unum' of Italy in linguistic terms (*De V.E.* I) is incompatible with the 'reductio ad unum' of the world in political-social terms (*Conv.* IV). The inference is questionable. It rests in part on the assumption of a considerable political basis or content in the first, linguistic unity of Italy, whereas it is clear from Dante's demonstration that this exists without the 'aula' or the 'curia'.[2] Yet even if we admit the possibility that Dante now saw a new justification of Latin as a universal medium coincident with universal empire, what has this necessarily changed in his linguistic outlook? Though he declared the vernacular more noble in *De V.E.*, he never cancelled Latin from his list any more than he claimed that one should write everything in vernacular (he did, after all, write *De V.E.* in

[1] *Purg.* xi.97ff:

> Così ha tolto l'uno a l'altro Guido
> la gloria de la lingua; e forse è nato
> chi l'uno e l'altro caccerà del nido. . . .

The example is worth bearing in mind for what is argued below regarding 'la lingua nostra'.

[2] 'È chiaro che, quando scrive il *De V.E.*, opera già fortemente in Dante il fatto politico . . .' (Vinay, p. 256). It is present, but should not be overstressed; certainly not as a motive behind Dante's image of linguistic unity of Italy. This exists without the 'aula' and the 'curia', which did not create the 'vulgare illustre', though they would provide its appropriate seat. The conditions of Frederick's court evidently, in Dante's view, encouraged its cultivation, but he does not say that it was 'born' there, or that its continued existence depended or depends on a similar political-social context.

Latin !); they are not mutually exclusive or incompatible, any more than Italy or France or Germany are incompatible with the Holy Roman Empire. Having discovered afresh the Roman mission and its poets, must Dante and everyone else now use only Latin? Vinay quotes in support of his thesis the passage about Cato in *Conv.* iv. xxvii.4, 'che non a sé, ma a la patria e a tutto lo mondo nato esser credea', and he underlines the last seven words, omitting conveniently to underline 'a la patria'. Did not Dante feel the same, and without feeling the need to sacrifice his 'italianità'? All the more so in that this 'italianità' is the nearest within the imperial concept to the survival of the glorious 'Latini'.

Mention of 'Latini' leads us finally to discuss the passage from *Purgatorio* which Vinay considers as a 'retractatio' on the subject of the vernacular. In Canto vii, 16ff. Sordello addresses Virgil in the following terms:

> O gloria de' Latin—disse—per cui
> mostrò ciò che potea la lingua nostra. . . .

Vinay comments:

Il volgare d'Italia è la lingua dei latini in quanto tali, la 'grammatica' è la lingua dei latini in quanto destinati da Dio a governare il mondo: l'uno e l'altro 'lingua nostra' per la congiunta italianità e universalità di Roma. Espressione oratoria. . . . di uno stato d'animo successivo al *De V.E.*, di una 'scoperta' non più linguistica ma storico-politica.

Whilst Dante refers elsewhere to Virgil as 'lo maggiore nostro poeta', and there is no difficulty in accepting the sense of Italian possession of this great poet, I am not sure that we are necessarily justified in concluding that 'lingua nostra' means exclusive Italian possession of Latin. I suggest that the phrase may be taken in another and more general sense, meaning 'all language'—with a sense akin to 'lo nostro sermone' in *Inf.* xxviii.1–6:

> Chi poria mai pur con parole sciolte
> dicer del sangue e de le piaghe a pieno
> ch'i'ora vidi, per narrar più volte?
> Ogne lingua per certo verria meno
> per *lo nostro sermone* e per la mente
> c'hanno a tanto comprender poco seno.

If this were accepted, it would enhance, not diminish, the praise of Virgil, because it would mean, not that Latin showed through him its supreme excellence, but that the gift of language found in his poem its highest expression.[1] Confirmation of this interpretation may also be found in *De V.E.* I. ii.1: 'Hec est nostra vera prima locutio. Non dico autem "nostra", ut et aliam sit esse locutionem quam hominis; nam eorum que sunt omnium soli homini datum est loqui, cum solum sibi necessarium fuerit'. It is true that Dante here speaks of vernacular. But we need not conclude that Sordello meant that Virgil wrote in vernacular; for besides this 'nostra vera prima locutio', 'est et inde alia locutio secundaria nobis quam Romani gramaticam vocaverunt'. This is still 'lingua nostra' in as much as we are human beings; and if it is less 'noble' in its origins, it embodies a superior tradition of art. On this plane Virgil demonstrates the highest perfection, and the specific identity of his medium is absorbed into the wider sense of human language.

It may be worth pressing the point a little farther at the risk of seeming pedantic. Why does Dante say: 'ciò che *potea* la lingua nostra'? If it means Latin, then it was and still is the same; or, following Vinay's line of argument, the 'coerenza del pensatore' should have persuaded Dante to write the *Comedy* in Latin; that is, if Latin could do that then with Virgil, it can and should still do it now for Dante. Perhaps it is seeking too much in the tense of 'potea', which may simply have been determined by 'mostrò' or by metrical considerations or both. But if 'lingua nostra' means human language however exalted by art, 'potea' takes on a historical sense in a different context, and the field is still open to whatever form that language takes, not narrowed to one. In other words, what greatness human language showed through Virgil using Latin, may still be paralleled through

---

[1] Cf. also ''l parlar nostro' in 'Amor che ne la mente mi ragiona', line 17, and relative commentary in *Conv.* IV. iv.11–13, and the numerous examples of 'nostro' in the sense of 'human' with other words like 'intelletto'. Everything depends in the interpretation of Sordello's words, on the assumed identity of 'Latin' with 'nostra'. The position of the possessive adj. after the noun has not necessarily a distinctive (i.e. selective) value; it varies considerably, without variation in sense, in Dante's usage.

Dante using Italian. Paralleled, perhaps, rather than challenged, for the *Aeneid* and the *Comedy* belong to different 'styles'. Yet some element of challenge to Latin poetry is not absent in Dante's poem (sometimes explicit, but more often implicit), and we should not underestimate its importance in appreciating his decision to use the vernacular for its composition.[1]

We should not deduce from the interruption of *De V.E.* and *Convivio*, and from Dante's ceasing to discuss further the relationship of Latin and Italian, that this was because Latin had in some sense triumphed. All the evidence of the *Comedy* and the pride of the poet are against it. His 'umanità' and the 'coerenza del pensatore' could not be more in harmony. On the particular question of nobility, Dante's thought in *Conv.* IV and *De V.E.* I appears consistent and complementary: the nobility of Man and the nobility of his language lie in their natural origins, and just as natural human virtue can be fostered and bring forth its fruits and aspire to greater perfection, so can the natural vernacular be trained and cultivated by art. The contradiction lies with *Conv.* I, which must have been written before he evolved such a theory about language or, having evolved it about human virtue, applied it to language. Whatever amendments he may have made in later years to details of his linguistic theory, what he says in *De V.E.* about the greater nobility of the vernacular (which does not mean the non-nobility of Latin) is his final explicit word on the subject.[2]

[1] The most obvious challenge is to Lucan and Ovid in *Inf.* xxv. 94ff.; the most evident sense of parity with the ancients is in Dante's acceptance among the poets in Limbo (*Inf.* iv. 102).

[2] This article represents substantially the first (and part of the second) of the three Barlow Lectures on Dante on the theme 'Dante and the Italian Language', delivered by me at University College, London, in May 1963. The third lecture was published, in Italian, under the title: 'Dante e la prosa volgare', in *Il Verri* (rivista di letteratura), no. 9 (August 1963), pp. 6–26.

4

Art and Artifice in the *Divina Commedia*[1]

ALFRED EWERT

IT would indeed be rash to seek to do more than adumbrate the question of Dante's technique or craftsmanship within the compass of a short paper: it cannot be dealt with satisfactorily unless one takes into account the whole of Dante's poetical works and his observations on language and the art of poetry. But for the limited purpose I have in mind, it may suffice to consider exclusively the *Commedia*. I think it is fair to say that, in sheer bulk, the greater part of what has been written about the *Divina Commedia* might stand unaltered if that great work had been written entirely in prose. There are of course many studies dealing with 'Dante the Poet'; they concern themselves for the most part with his poetic conception (or conceptions), with the evocative quality of his words, the splendour of his images, the aptness of his similes. All these are of the essence of poetry, but they leave out what is the most distinctive and essential element of poetry—its music and rhythm, or (to express it metaphorically) the rhythmic throb, the echoes and reverberations of living poetry, whether conveyed in the disposition and nature of the rhymes or in the more subtle and less obvious ordering of the internal elements of the individual lines; and that is not my opinion, but Dante's own, expressed, for example, in the *De Vulgari Eloquentia* (II. iv.18–20) to the effect that poetry, 'si poesim recte consideremus', is 'nihil aliud . . . quam fictio rethorica musicaque composita', i.e. 'a rhetorical composition set to music'. Unfortunately, such questions of form have nearly always been answered by means of elaborate analyses of the so-called rules governing rhyme, disposition of stresses,

---

[1] This essay is adapted from a paper read to the Oxford Dante Society at a meeting held on 28 May 1946, in Trinity College.

syllable-count, stanza-types, etc., analyses which do not tell us—indeed, I suppose it is not their job to tell us—the place of 'rules' in the act of poetic creation of a poet like Dante, though they may throw considerable light on the gestatory processes of the mere versifier.

The act of poetic creation—and I use the term only of the sort of creation which gave us the *Divina Commedia*—is a mystery, a 'selva oscura', in which 'la diritta via' is hard to find. Only a poet could begin to explain it to us, and it has seldom been more than tentatively described by even the most intellectual and self-critical or self-observant poets. And this should not surprise us, since we have the greatest difficulty in analysing the process underlying even the simplest utterance of our day-to-day language and are reduced to describing what we consider it to be by very rough analogies and metaphors, as when we talk of sound-pictures or verbal images in the speaker's mind. When dealing with the process of poetic creation we are in the presence of a subtle transmutation, a sort of synthetizing process, the elements of which are as insubstantial echoes, transmitted—some from afar off in the haze of the poet's past experience, some from more immediate impulses conveyed through one or other of the senses or through several interacting upon each other: a scent suggesting a sound, a word or a sound suggesting a sensation, that sensation suggesting a word, and so on. Many of these echoes sound in the poet's mind unbidden, and they often present themselves already invested with their verbal counterparts. But, intervening in this synthetizing process— before it begins, while it is going on, or after it has taken place—we have the will of the poet, his design and conscious purpose. I am not now speaking of such things as the mere disposition of the cantos, but of the creation of the many immortal lines of the *Commedia*. It is with this intervention, to use a convenient though somewhat misleading term, that I think scholars and critics of Dante might, to our advantage, have occupied themselves more directly.

I have purposely refrained from speaking of *conscious* intervention, because it seems to me quite misleading to distinguish merely between conscious and unconscious, when in fact it is a question of infinitely varying degrees of consciousness. I prefer to make a broad distinction between that which comes unbidden to the poet and that which comes at his bidding (or which he does by design). It is with the latter that I am here more particularly concerned, and I ask myself the question: 'How far or in what degree did Dante, when inditing the *Commedia,* proceed of or by design?' Everything we know about Dante would predispose us to answer: 'very far' and 'to a very high degree', and to conclude that he is definitely to be classed with those poets whom Schiller described as *sentimental* as opposed to those whom he called *naiv*. When Dante, in the *De V.E.* (ii. iv.66–73), after advising the poet to 'drink of Helicon, adjust his strings and boldly take his plectrum and begin to ply it', adds: 'but it is in the exercise of the needful caution and discernment (*discretio*) that the real difficulty lies; for this can never be attained without strenuous efforts of genius, constant practising of the art, and the habit of the sciences,' there can be no doubt of his meaning. And when he says at the beginning of *Par.* xxv:

> Se mai continga che il poema sacro,
> Al quale ha posto mano e cielo e terra,
> Sì che m'ha fatto per più anni macro,
> Vinca la crudeltà . . .

it seems to me legitimate to conclude that he does not refer merely to the studied elaboration of his theme, but to the sustained effort (repeated at a constant level over the months and years) required to overcome the difficulties imposed by the form he had chosen, to the technical virtuosity demanded by his medium and his own imperious demands upon himself.[1]

It may well be held that the threefold division: *Inferno—Purgatorio—Paradiso* is merely dictated by the nature of his subject, reinforced by what might almost be called Dante's ternary cast of mind or trichotomous instinct; but that the three cantiche should be so nearly of equal length (*Inf.* 4720 lines, *Purg.* 4755, *Par.* 4758) is surely not the result of some rhythmical ebb and flow of inspiration. If there were

[1] S. Breglia, *Poesia e struttura nella Divina Commedia* (Genova, 1934).

any doubt, it would be dispelled by the closing lines of the
Purgatorio:

> Ma perchè piene son tutte le carte
> Ordite a questa Cantica seconda,
> Non mi lascia più ir lo fren dell'arte;

which means, if not 'I have exhausted the ration of parch-
ment allotted to this cantica', at least: 'this cantica has now
attained the length required by the symmetry of the work
as I have planned it'. Similarly, no one will question the
conscious design underlying the division of each cantica into
33 cantos, with an introductory one for the first cantica. As
for the length of the individual cantos, we observe that to
some extent there is obvious calculation in that, for example,
in the *Inferno*, after two introductory cantos, Ante-Hell is
disposed of in Canto III, the First Circle in Canto IV, the
Second Circle in Canto V, the Third in Canto VI, and
similarly in other parts of the *Commedia*; but I need hardly
add that to this there are exceptions, Canto VII treating of
both the Fourth and the beginning of the Fifth Circle, &c.
This might suggest that Dante, if he did not simply follow
his poetic inspiration of the moment, at any rate did not
allow any preconceived pattern to inhibit him from enlarg-
ing upon those sins and abuses which particularly kindled
his reprobation. This he must have envisaged and allowed
for before finally fixing his plan, and the element of artifice
expresses itself clearly in the fact that there is so little
variation in the length of the cantos.

It may be recalled that the average length of the cantos
is, in the *Inferno* 139 lines, *Purgatorio* 144, *Paradiso* 144·1,
and in the whole of the *Commedia* 142·3. The shortest cantos
(all in the *Inferno*) are: two of 115 and one of 124, all the
rest being of over 130 lines. The longest cantos are: one of
160 (*Purg.*) and one of 157 (*Inf.*), all the rest being under
155 lines. There is here clearly, if not preconceived plan,
at any rate conscious design.

Coming now to the elements of the canto from the
technical point of view, we are first of all concerned with
Dante's choice and handling of the terza rima. According
to Bembo, this was first employed by Dante. Since his day

various sources have been suggested, including the three-line stanza employed by the French poet Rutebeuf (*ca.* 1250–1285). It is possible, and one might even say probable, that Dante was familiar with Rutebeuf's work, but the tercet which the latter employed for parts of his *Miracle de Theophile* and for his *Complainte* and one or two other poems, consists of two eight-syllable lines followed by a four-syllable line, and the rhyme scheme is *aab, bbc, ccd,* etc. The *Complainte* closes with an incomplete tercet, the last short line being omitted:

> Monseignor qui est filz de roi
> Mon dit et ma complainte envoi,
>   Qu'il m'est mestiers,
> Qu'il m'a aidié moult volentiers:
> Ce est li bons quens de Poitiers
>   Et de Toulouse;
> Il savra bien que cil goulouse
> Qui si faitement se doulouse.[1]

This cannot be said to be a particularly inspiring model for Dante to have imitated. It is more likely, as suggested by J. S. P. Tatlock,[2] that Dante got the idea from the sestet of the thirteenth-century Italian sonnet as practised by himself, for example, in the twelfth sonnet of the *Vita Nuova*:

> E se venite da tant pietate,
>   Piacciavi di restar qui meco alquanto,
> E qual che sia di lei, nol mi celate:
> Io veggio gli occhi vostri c'hanno pianto,
>   E veggiovi tornar sì sfigurate,
> Che'l cor mi trema di vederne tanto;

which here, and generally, has a definite break in the middle and therefore presents all the features of the terza rima except that it lacks a new rhyme in the last line but one which would rhyme in its turn with lines 1 and 3 of a following terzina.[3]

---

[1] *La Complainte Rutebeuf*, in *Œuvres Complètes de Rutebeuf*, p.p. E. Faral et Julia Bastin (Paris, Picard, 1959), i. 558.

[2] 'Dante's *terza rima*', *P.M.L.A.* li (1936), pp. 895–903.

[3] Other possible sources and influences were examined in detail by Professor T. B. W. Reid in a paper read to the Oxford Dante Society at a meeting held on 18 February 1964, in Magdalen College.

Of one thing we may be quite sure: the choice was not made lightly. It may have been made because of the indisputable potentialities of the form, at least as practised by Dante: a combination of repose (duality of rhyme) and movement (i.e. constant anticipation in the middle of a terzina of a new pair of rhymes). Contemplation and narrative progression are implied in it, and both are exploited to the full by Dante, a fact which is thrown into proper relief if we compare the use made of the terza rima by later poets. Each terzina forms an entity, but in such a way as to secure at the same time a continuity of narrative, and Dante therefore frequently makes an effective use of an overflow from one terzina to the next, a practice which later came to be branded as a mistake. Compare particularly *Purg.* xxx.34–39 or *Par.* xxiii.1–15, with their striking effect of a symphonic crescendo. Alternatively, he may use successive terzine to present two elements of a comparison (*Inf.* i. 22–27). That these effects are the result of a virtuosity acquired by dint of 'caution', 'discernment' and 'practice', and not merely of the spontaneous warbling of a divinely inspired songster, hardly requires demonstration.

Other considerations, such as mnemonic convenience, may also have weighed with Dante, but the reason advanced by Tatlock certainly operates alongside these and may well have been the clinching argument. Tatlock pointed out that the terze rime make an interpolation virtually impossible, that is to say impossible without repeating the same rhyme within a canto at a comparatively short interval. Against internal omissions Dante was completely protected. Another consequence is that later insertions by Dante himself were made impossible without extensive recasting, which fact supports again the conclusion that he designed very carefully, not only the cantiche but also the individual cantos, before ever inditing them.

On the subject of rhymes a good deal has been written—about their variety, their aptness and so on; and it is the rhymes that have furnished the most reliable evidence for a study of Dante's language. Within the line we are faced by the fundamental difficulty that we constantly find in one or more MSS an archaic or dialectal or Latinized word which in other MSS appears in a different form (which may be a good standard Tuscan form). If the syllable-count furnishes no clue (as is frequently the case), we cannot, in the present state of our knowledge, be certain which is Dante's reading; and, even if we could establish which form he would normally use, we could not be sure that aesthetic considerations might not impel him to use, in the particular instance, another form selected from the variant forms available to him (*fuoco* or *foco*, and the like). This eclectic procedure is, in fact, what we find his practice to have been in respect of rhyme. It is largely on the basis of the rhyme that statistics such as those of Zingarelli are established.[1] These show that, roughly speaking, the non-Tuscan features appear in the following proportions:

	Inf.	*Purg.*	*Par.*	*Total*
Phonetic and Morphological Latinisms	40	49	84	173
Lexicographical Latinisms	34	41	187	262
Semantic Latinisms	19	11	28	58
	93	101	299	493

Gallicisms (French and Provençal)	*ca.* 75
Dialectalisms	*ca.* 41
Misc. (Greek, Hebrew, etc.)	*ca.* 15

These statistics may serve to indicate the existence of certain non-Florentine elements in considerable numbers, though less considerable if we subtract those words which, like 'pape Satan aleppe' (*Inf.* vii.1), should be read, so to speak, in inverted commas.

How are these non-Florentine elements to be interpreted? Some scholars have maintained that such uses of dialectal, foreign or borrowed words (or forms of words) in the rhyme are licences of the poet's own, which might be regarded as almost tantamount to a charge of cheating. But there is

[1] N. Zingarelli, 'Parole e forme della *Divina Commedia* aliene dal dialetto fiorentino', *Studi di Filologia Romanza*, i (1885), pp. 1–202; particularly p. 107. See also A. Schiaffini, 'Note sul colorito dialettale della *Divina Commedia*', *Studi Danteschi*, xiii (1929), pp. 32–45.

another interpretation, which I would relate to a view I ventured to place before the Society in a previous paper.[1] It is that, when Dante wrote, there already existed a partly standardized language, with what amounted to a Tuscan base, but admitting (as modern Italian still does) a great number of dialectal and other variants. It is in this imperfectly and unacknowledged standard language, used by a limited class of the population, that Dante found these variants or alternatives currently used. They were not dragged in by him to suit the occasion: they were present, if not in the language of the ordinary citizen of Florence, at least in that of the persons with whom Dante constantly associated, or at the very least in the literary language of his time.

If it is therefore untrue that Dante merely dragged in these variants from the dialects, from French, from Provençal, from Latin, from archaic texts, it is equally false, but for other reasons, to suggest that his rhymes invariably came to him unbidden, and equally unjust to Dante to endow him with an effortless facility. We must admit the probability of varying degrees of effort or effortlessness, ranging from completely unbidden rhyme to the consciously contrived, the latter being particularly found among the scattered *versi tronchi*: *Inf.* xxxii.26 (*Osteric*), 28 (*Tambernic*), 30 (*cric*), etc.

The subject of the structure of the line and its internal disposition is not to be broached lightly by those whose native language is not Italian, and yet it is not to be burked if one wishes to achieve a proper appreciation of Dante's craftsmanship. There is, of course, no doubt whatever that every single line of the *Commedia*, as committed to posterity by Dante, satisfied his ear on the score of syllable-count. It is a fact that, when discussing (in *De V.E.* ii. v.26) the ten-syllable line of Giraut de Borneil:

Ara ausirez encabalitz cantars

and the ten-syllable line of Thibaut de Navarre:

De fin Amor si vient sen et bonté,

[1] Since published under the title 'Dante's Theory of Language', *Modern Language Review*, xxxv (1940), pp. 355–66.

Dante perversely makes them into eleven-syllable lines by insisting that, in the first case, the final *-rs* counts as part of the next syllable (understood), and in the second case, 'if the accent [of *bonté*] and its cause [*-té-*<*tatem?*] be considered, the line will be found to have eleven syllables'; but that fact will not mislead anyone, and it is not quite so perverse as might appear.[1] Without becoming involved in that most vexed question of all: what is a syllable?, we may safely affirm that, whatever rules, exceptions and accommodations the reader may have to apply in order to make all the lines of the *Commedia* 'scan', Dante conceived and articulated them—even if only *sotto voce*—as lines consisting of eleven phonetic units, and intended them to produce acoustically the identical effect. That is to say, they are to be read not word by word or phrase by phrase, but line by line, each line as a whole, with the rhyme as the signal though not necessarily marking a halt or an interruption in the flow of successive lines.

From Dante's practice certain rules can be deduced, including the permissible licences in such matters as hiatus, etc. Many of these Dante undoubtedly learned during his apprenticeship, although they may have ceased to be 'rules' for him, except in the sense of organic laws; e.g. the rule that the fifth syllable must not bear the stress—to which rule it would be difficult to find a genuine exception. But it is reasonable to suppose that yet others, no doubt a small number, continued to be genuine rules applied by him more or less consciously.

As for the rhythm of the line, some of the 'rules' evolved by critics have been little short of fantastic. Some of their affirmations are clearly inspired by such considerations as the rules of classical prosody or, in the case of English and German critics, by the Germanic system of regularly recurring stresses. For example, Tozer, in his chapter on the 'Metre of the Divina Commedia' appended to Moore's *Textual Criticism*, tells us categorically to scan the opening line: 'Nel mézzo dél cammín di nóstra víta'. The application of such 'rules' for purposes of textual criticism would have

---

[1] Cf. Mario Casella, 'Endecasillabi di dodici sillabe?', *Studi Danteschi*, xxiv (1939), pp. 79–109.

disastrous consequences since it is manifest that the internal structure of the line is not regular or standardizable and that it is even misleading to speak of a caesura as some critics do.[1] The basis of the rhythm is the *ordinary* rhythm of spoken Italian, in which the degree of stress is determined by the existence of tonic syllables in individual words or by the stressing of particular words according to their function in the sentence. And here one may grant that Dante had a special advantage in the *volgare illustre* which he so justifiably exalted; but this advantage is reduced to its proper perspective when we consider that it has not prevented many execrable lines being contrived by many poets.

Superimposed on this ordinary rhythm are what we may call rhetorical, emphatic or emotional stresses, which give a special prominence to syllables that already bear an ordinary stress, and this will be found to be the normal effect in Dante's lines. But it may occasionally happen (and therefore with all the more effect) that the emotional stress falls on a syllable which in normal speech would not be stressed—to say nothing of so-called 'licences', when the accent is made to fall on a syllable which in normal standard Tuscan should never bear a stress (*piéta* for *pietà*), nor of other licences which are or have been common practice in Italian poetry and which are clearly employed by Dante *en connaissance de cause*.

It is in the marvellous concordance between the nature of his rhythm (i.e. the distribution of these stresses) and the emotional state of the poet and the emotional content of the line that the transcending genius of Dante lies. How much of this is the result of design? If we mean by design the observance of pre-existing rules, the answer is surely: nothing. And there is a serious danger in any attempt to identify particular types of rhythm (iambic, dactylic, etc.)

[1] For a discussion of this whole question, see Martha Amrein-Widmer's *Rhythmus als Ausdruck inneren Lebens in Dantes Divina Commedia* (Zürich, Rascher, 1932) which, in spite of exaggerations and other shortcomings, approaches the subject from the right angle and contains many pertinent observations and analyses. F. D'Ovidio's *Versificazione romanza: poetica e poesia medioevale* (vols. ix–x of *Opere di F. D'Ovidio* (Napoli, Guida, 1932)), remains authoritative on the question of versification. See, further, the short bibliography in Amrein-Widmer, pp. 139–140.

with particular types of sensation or with different moods, just as it is wrong to attach, *in principle*, a particular significance or evocative power to particular vowels and consonants (e.g. lightness and swiftness to the so-called light vowels *i* and *e*, heaviness and sluggishness to the dark vowels *o* and *u*). What is decisive in such a case is the accumulation of such sounds, or the context. For example, one must concede the 'light-producing' effect of the repetition of the sound *i* in a line like *Par.* xxx.47: 'Gli spiriti visivi, sì che priva . . .', or the 'caressing' effect of the consonant *l* in *Par.* xxv.5: 'Del bello ovil, dov' io dormii agnello . . .' If we mean by design a more or less conscious effort to induce in the reader, by technical means, the same complex of thought and emotion which the poet felt and wished to convey, then the answer must surely be that not all the lines sprang fully-fashioned from the mind of the poet, that in many instances a second thought was better than a first, that a more effective way of ordering the elements of his lines suggested itself to him; in a word, that he concluded, thanks to 'caution' and 'discernment', that the acoustic and other effects he intended would be better ensured by the second rendering. And in this connexion one might point to instances where words would appear to have been added by the poet which in respect of matter could not unfairly be described as padding and which may well have been adopted to satisfy the demands of form, whether for the sake of rhythm or merely syllable-count; for example, one might be tempted to say as much of a whole line like *Inf.* i.30. But that is a kind of critical activity which, besides being hazardous, is perhaps best dismissed as presumptuous pedantry.

Leaving aside, then, all forms of pedantry, we may conclude that while the broad lines of the different cantos and the lineaments of the successive terzine suffered no material revision at the hands of the Poet, the number of changes within the line may well have been very considerable, and that this may account for many of the vast number of minor variants presented by the manuscripts. It is quite possible that in respect of these apparently insignificant variations we have to do, not with 'corruptions' inflicted on the author's definitive text, but with traces of a first version, a second version, and possibly more, all lost to us. This would make the attainment of a genuinely authoritative edition even more of a will-of-the-wisp than it has hitherto proved to be and would suggest that the application of rationalized and mechanical criteria can never take us more than part of the way to this goal.

The extraordinary virtuosity of the poet in the single aspect of his art represented by the disposition of the internal elements of the line can be illustrated from every page, and perhaps with special pertinence from the famous Francesca passage in *Inf.* v. I need hardly repeat what has in effect been said before: that we have here much more than a story designed to underline the reprehensible nature of sensual adulterous love and a touching tale marvellously told. The spell which these lines have cast over successive generations of readers is due almost entirely to the extraordinary beauty of the sheer ordering of the vowels and consonants and accents, giving the impression of a direct and immediate rendering of some profound emotional experience of the poet, vividly recalled from the past and finding expression almost without the need for mere narrative. But it might be more illuminating to take as an example some other passage less heavily charged with memories and yet characteristic, such as *Purg.* xiv.127–35:

> Noi sapevám che quell' ánime cáre
> Ci sentívano andár: però tacéndo
> Facevan nói del cammín confidáre.
> Poi fummo fátti sóli procedéndo,
> Fólgore pàrve, quando l'áer fénde,
> Vóce che giùnse d'incóntra, dicéndo:
> 'Anciderámmi qualúnque m'appténde;'
> E fuggí, come tuón che si dilégua,
> Se súbito la núvola scoscénde.[1]

Through the mouth of Guido del Duca, Dante has just denounced the vices of the dwellers by the Arno and the

---

[1] One of a large number of passages discussed by Dr. Amrein-Widmer (on pp. 84–86). I have indicated by means of an acute accent the syllables which bear a rhythmical stress and mark the end of each of the constituent rhythmical elements of the line.

degeneracy of the great families in the cities of Romagna. The flame of indignation which burns in those preceding lines has died down and the opening lines of our passage are in a mood of tender recollection inspired by Guido and his companion: and this is conveyed by the rhythm, almost without regard to the semantic content of the words, all three lines being of virtually the same pattern (accents on 4—7—10; 3—6—10): 'Noi sapevam. . . .' Then a warning note of apprehension in 130, with a suggestion of anxiety ('Poi fummo . . .') in a slightly different rhythm (4—6—10), and then without warning the wrath of the poet flaring up again in the prediction of retribution in l. 131 ('Folgore . . .'), the rhythm 1—8—10 (with a fourth secondary stress on 'parve', reinforced by the f—f alliteration; the hiatus 'a-er' almost suggesting the cleaving of the air, a hiatus which some editors have been so undiscerning as to eliminate pedantically by reading 'aere', which some of the manuscripts offer. Note particularly the striking effect produced by two stresses in quick succession: 'l'áer fénde'. The next line (132) maintains this with a slight change of rhythm suggesting an abatement ('Voce che' . . .), only to reach its climax in the first part of the next line with its extraordinary effect: 'Anciderammi', followed by 'qualunque m'apprende'—the voice of Cain beginning to recede; then 'E fuggì', the complete and—as we read—apparent inevitability of which should not lead us to suppose that a lesser poet would necessarily have thought to use just this word. Then the trailing off of Cain's voice in the distance suggested by the rhythm of the last two lines and the concordant effect of the two 'dark' back diphthongs *uo* and *ua*, the first stressed, the second aptly unstressed.—This crude pedestrian attempt to follow, on the ground, the empyrean flight of the poet will not, I trust, have defeated its own purpose, which was to attempt at least some illustration in support of the general observations made above.

    Considered from this technical point of view, the *Paradiso* represents the final and supreme effort of Dante. If admirers of the poet do not more often read the *Paradiso*, is it perhaps because they are inclined to read it too much as a treatise or an allegory, and not as Dante's last and definitive words as a poet? And if we must confess our failure to follow him here, are we perhaps not in precisely the same case as those who surrender themselves to the enchantment of Beethoven's early quartets, and attribute to him and not to themselves their failure to follow him in the later? Or, if we must transfer some of the onus to Dante, may we perhaps say that Dante's vision of Paradise was so dazzling that he did not quite realize how difficult it would be for his readers to appreciate the refinements of his formal rendering of it?

5

Bridges and Dante

CESARE FOLIGNO

D R. ROBERT BRIDGES (he disliked being called doctor) attended as a guest the sixty-ninth meeting of the Oxford Dante Society on 30 May 1899 when Mr. Herbert Warren (as he then was) read a paper on *Gray and Dante*; and, unless my memory betrays me, it was Sir Herbert Warren who, when Bridges was appointed to succeed Alfred Austin as Poet Laureate, suggested that it would be fitting to approach him with a view to ascertaining whether he would be willing to become a member of the Dante Society. Of their friendly relations there is evidence in the lines Bridges addressed to Warren on his election to the presidency of Magdalen College in 1885; he wrote:

> Such tribute, Warren, as fond poets pay
> For generous esteem, I write, not more
> Enhearten'd than my need is . . .

adding a wish fortunately to be realized:

> I bid your presidency a long reign.[1]

The 'generous esteem' this poetical 'tribune' was intended to pay had been presumably expressed on the publication of a book of verse; whether *Poems* (Daniel Press, 1884) or *Eros and Psyche* (London, Bell, 1885) or even an isolated poem, it is now impossible to decide.

The election did not follow immediately upon the first suggestion because of the unwillingness of the Poet Laureate to undertake entertaining and addressing the Society, and also because of some hesitation Dr. Paget Toynbee, the Society's secretary and 'dictator', felt. He had slightly

[1] *Later Poems*, No. 10.

relaxed some of the almost liturgical regulations Canon
Moore had enforced, by allowing members to smoke and
to wear dinner jackets at meetings instead of the full evening
dress that had been previously obligatory; he fancied that
an 'active member' might prove more useful than an
'honorary' one, however famous, and felt unable to discern
adequate evidence of a deep interest in Dante in such writings of Bridges as he had read. Practically all the members
were in favour from the first, and one would not be far
wrong in supposing that Professor W. P. Ker and Professor
J. W. Mackail proved the most effective agents in dispelling
Toynbee's doubts. The election was triumphantly unanimous, and from 1915 onwards the Poet Laureate attended
meetings fairly often, though he never, or only very seldom,
took part in the discussion.

It was possibly on this account that some vestige of
doubt still lurked in Toynbee's mind as a mannerism of his
appeared to show. In his delightful account of the Oxford
Dante Society after the First World War,[1] Professor E. F.
Jacob recalls Toynbee's mannerism of always alluding to
him as the 'Junior Member'. Yet this presumably echoed a
more significant and earlier mannerism. When reading out,
in the order of their Society seniority, the names of the
members who had attended the previous meeting, on coming
to the end of the list, Toynbee would pause, draw a kind of
sigh or rather a groan, and, in a voice one octave lower than
his normal one, add: 'and . . . the Poet Laureate, (*dimin-
uendo*) Honorary Member'. I do not remember his ever
dealing in this manner with the name of President of
Magdalen who was also an honorary member. His perform-
ance at times caused the eyes of W. P. Ker to twinkle
behind his glasses, and the Poet himself to look amused.

In point of fact, unless something has escaped me, only
once did Bridges deal with Dante in his prose writings
('Dante in English Literature', *T.L.S.*, 24 June 1909:
Prose Works, vol. viii): and even then, mainly indirectly
and by linking him with Milton, as though he were really
impressed by Dante's greatness merely in so far as it is
reflected in Milton. It would, however, be rash to reach

---

[1] *English Miscellany* No. 9 (Rome, 1958), p. 200.

such a conclusion without searching for other evidence and especially through his poems; for it would be inconceivable for a man who placed poetry above all other arts, and who from his youth had diligently endeavoured to master the technicalities of his craft, not to be impressed by the scope and power of Dante's achievement. And though he may have lacked an intimate familiarity with Italian, he could not fail to be struck by what has been described as the 'inevitability' of Dante's choice of words. There may be parts of the works of the Florentine poet at which Bridges never cast a glance. He almost prided himself on the capriciousness of his taste, and one can well imagine him to have ignored the epistles, the *Monarchia*, maybe even chapters of the *Convivio*; but references to Dante, particularly to some sections of his works, occur very early. Early of course in so far as Bridges allowed, for he meticulously destroyed or recast everything he had written before he was well advanced in his medical studies.

It is in no case easy to trace definite reminiscences of other poets in Bridges' verse; their echoes are fleeting and evanescent, and one gathers the impression that he may seldom have looked up passages in books, and mostly trusted to his memory, reproducing the words of other poets not necessarily as they had been written, but as they were retained in his mind or refashioned by it. There are passages that lead forcibly to such an hypothesis.

Bridges, who had visited France, Germany, Italy, and the Near East and who possessed an observant eye, seldom allowed the names of places and references to them to appear in his verse or to be retained there if they had at first slipped from his quill, the only writing instrument he used. An exception may be pointed out, however, in sonnet No. 17 of *The Growth of Love* in which he mentions Florence, calling her 'the city of Dante'; another in sonnet No. 18 of the same series, a sonnet that had already appeared in 1876,[1] where, looking down upon Florence from the convent

---

[1] Excluding the edition LXXIX *sonnets* (Daniel Press, 1889), reproduced in America and in black letter in 1890, the sets to be considered are XXIV *Sonnets* (Bumpus, 1876), and the final edition, *Poetical Works*, vol. i (Smith, Elder & Co., 1898, also Oxford University Press, 1913).

of San Miniato, after mentioning Giotto and Michelangelo, he adds:

> And Dante, gravest poet, her much wrong'd son.

Sonnet No. 23, which was No. VII among those published in 1876, begins with a line the swing of which irresistibly recalls the first line of a sonnet in the *Vita Nuova* (para. xl, sections 9–10[1]) and the movement and rhythm of which, though not its meaning, seem to be echoed in Bridges:

> O weary pilgrims, chanting on your way,
> That turn your eyes to all the peaks that shine. . . .

Dante wrote:

> Deh peregrini che pensosi andate,
> forse di cosa che non v'è presente. . . .

Sonnet No. 69 of *The Growth of Love*, which was No. XVIII in the 1876 edition, the last of the series in each case, also calls for attention. It is a paraphrase of the Lord's Prayer, and, though there are no other prayers in this series of Sonnets, would not necessarily remind one that the same prayer is paraphrased by Dante in *Purg.* xi.1–21, namely in twenty-one lines. Was Bridges tempted to challenge comparison with the older poet, famed for his concision, by using fourteen lines only? Verbal similarities would prove of little help; it should be noted, however, that the second quatrain read in the 1876 edition:

> Perfect Thy kingdom, which our souls await,
> That looking down on earth Thou may'st approve
> Our worship and obedience, as above
> Thine angel service we would emulate.

It was altered in the 1898 and following editions to:

> Perfect Thy Kingdom in our passing state,
> That here on earth Thou may'st as well approve
> Our service, as Thou ownest theirs above,
> Whose joy we echo and in pain await.

Dante reads:

[1] Quotations from Dante are taken from the *Testo Critico*.

Vegna ver noi la pace del tuo regno,
ché noi ad essa non potem da noi,
s'ella non vien, con tutto nostro ingegno.

Come del tuo voler li angeli tuoi
fan sacrificio a te cantando osanna,
cosí facciano li uomini de' suoi.   (vv.7–12)

Angels are not mentioned by Matthew or Luke; it was Dante who brought them in, as if they were the only or principal inhabitants of heaven. Bridges 'Thine angel' seems to echo Dante's 'li angeli', and if the actual word 'angel' is avoided in the later form of the quatrain, the words 'Theirs above' with what follows can only refer to angels and saints. Is it not permissible to imagine that Bridges had Dante's words in mind in 1876, and that later, wishing to keep closer to the Gospels or not to be definite in eventual additions, he changed the reading of his lines? This inference may appear to be rather farfetched at first sight, but less so if one takes into consideration the necessarily restricted limits consistent with a paraphrase.

At all events, that Bridges was familiar with the *Divina Commedia* when he was producing some of his earlier works is attested by the inscription of a line *l'anima semplicetta che sa nulla* (*Purg*. xvi.88) on the title page of his delightful version of Apuleius, as though he meant to prepare his readers for the naïve simplemindedness of Psyche. *Eros and Psyche* was published in 1885.

Hard to define is the connexion of sonnet No. 38 of the *Growth of Love* with Dante's sonnet *Guido, i' vorrei* (*Rime* LII). The differences are so marked that only a careful comparison can help one to see the similarity. Bridges wrote:

An idle June day on the sunny Thames,
Floating or rowing as our fancy led,
Now in the high beams basking as we sped,
Now in green shade gliding by the mirror'd stems;
    By lock and weir and isle, and many a spot
Of memoried pleasures, glad with strength and skill,
Friendship, good wine and mirth, that serve not ill
The heavenly Muse, tho' she require them not;

> I would have life—thou saidst—all as this day,
> Simple enjoyment calm in its excess,
> With not a grief to cloud, and not a ray
> Of passion overhot my peace to oppress;
> With no ambition to reproach delay,
> Nor rapture to disturb its happiness.

And Dante:

> Guido, i' vorrei che tu e Lapo ed io
> fossimo presi per incantamento
> e messi in un vasel, ch'ad ogni vento
> per mare andasse al voler vostro e mio;
> sí che fortuna od altro tempo rio
> non ci potesse dare impedimento,
> anzi, vivendo sempre in un talento,
> di stare insieme crescesse 'l disio.
>
> E monna Vanna e monna Lagia poi
> con quella ch'è sul numer de le trenta
> con noi ponesse il buono incantatore;
> e quivi ragionar sempre d'amore,
> e ciascuna di lor fosse contenta,
> sí come i' credo che saremmo noi.

What is a message in Dante becomes, with Bridges, a reported dialogue; the boat is the same, swept along by friendly breezes or by the stream; more dreamlike the landscape in Dante; strength and skill are substituted for *incantamento*; the mood of enchanted idleness is the same; Dante is not thinking of the Muse, only of love; no woman is mentioned by Bridges, but the speaker in the ninth line is obviously a woman. Not only is the general mood similar, but the last six lines of the English sonnet are clearly reminiscent of Dante's, particularly in their melodious rhythm.

A reminiscence of some of the last lines of *Paradiso* in *Demeter*, ll. 1054 and following may appear less easy to recognize when one scrutinizes these two passages, than when one reads them through listening to their sound and overlooking some discrepancies:

> Nay, the things
> Not to be told, because there are no words
> Of gods or men to paint the inscrutable

...... I saw
The meaning and the reason of all things,
All at a glance, and in that glance perceiv'd
The origin of all things. . . .[1]

The omissions—it must be confessed—are a clear case of faking evidence, for Persephone is pointing to evil as the origin of all things and Dante, on the contrary, to the very essence of divinity:

Nel suo profondo vidi che s'interna
legato con amore in un volume,
ciò che per l'universo si squaderna;
  sustanze e accidenti e lor costume,
quasi conflati insieme, . . .[2]

It is difficult to single out expressions that are really similar; the general meaning—we know—is opposite. Despite this, one does feel a peculiar kind of likeness. Perhaps Dante himself could help us. He was able to perceive the character of a movement, let us say its manner and quality, irrespective of its direction:

Levava li occhi miei bagnati in pianti,
e vedea, che parean pioggia di manna,
li angeli che tornavan suso in cielo,
e una nuvoletta avean davanti. . . .[3]

The solemn, quiet upward soaring of the angels towards heaven in the wake of a cloud, and the soft beneficial rain of manna falling towards the earth, are identified, just as the fullness of vision in *Demeter*, merely because of its fullness, may be inspired by that of Dante in *Paradiso* irrespective of what Persephone and Dante are contemplating.

Possibly the same standard of perfection that rendered Bridges so meticulous in aiming at the proper spelling of English words and their pronunciation caused him, perhaps instinctively, to avoid uttering foreign words and quoting foreign verse. An incident occurs to me that illustrates this attitude of his. At a Worcester College garden party following the Encaenia I happened to be talking to Solomon

[1] Act III.1054–9.   [2] *Par.* xxxiii.85–89.
[3] *Vita nuova*, xxiii.25, Canzone, *Donna pietosa*, 57–60.

Reinach, who had received an honorary degree and who was rather reluctant to speak English. Bridges passed by. His noble features, his figure, and his carriage, at all times striking, were particularly so when he was seen in full academic dress against a sun-lit background of trees and lawns. Reinach asked me about him. When approached, Bridges looked down at the short, rotund Frenchman with a frank welcoming smile, bowed deeply; then sprang suddenly erect, and, facing the sky, his resonant voice louder because of the initial impediment, he roared: 'Je parle français horriblement', and despite the rich rolling of the liquids, he spoke truly. He turned on his heel and strode across the lawn, his gown and hood fluttering in his wake.

I was reminded of this incident when, not many weeks later, at Chilswell, in his rock-garden, he uttered a few words from the *Divina Commedia*; the only Italian quotation I ever heard him make. He was urging that style and the choice of words need not necessarily depend on the meaning; that the same idea can be effectively expressed in different ways, and said: 'Your Dante has *sta come torre* and *lascia pur grattar* and meant the same thing.' He kept his quotations as short as possible and broke them off; his Italian pronunciation was no better than his French, and I was barely able to recognize the passages (*Purg.* v.14 and *Par.* xvii.129); but his totally unexpected Dante 'outburst' struck me as significant. I did not argue the point. I should never have dreamt of contradicting him. To me his personality was overwhelming. To watch him; to listen to him; to observe the crystal-clear and occasionally staggering originality of what he said were privileges to enjoy; and besides, I was well aware that any doubt or objection of mind would have been swept away by him as pedantic. I had heard him quote Dante by heart; that was enough. At the time it was almost a revelation to me; and in a way it may help one to realize how Dantean reminiscences came about in his verse.

Some are puzzling. There is a tantalizing dialogue between A. and B. in *La Gloire de Voltaire* (*Later Poems*, No. 13), in which A. praises and B. belittles Voltaire. B. says in his third speech:

> And think of those foredoom'd in Dante's pit,
> Who, sunk at the bottom of the loathly slough,
> Made the black mud up-bubble with their sighs;
> And all because they were unkind to Mirth,
> And went with smoky heart and gloomy brow
> The while they lived upon the pleasant earth
> In the sweet air that rallies to the sun,
> And ne'er so much as smiled or gave God thanks

A. replies; and B. rejoins, asking for no truce between Voltaire

> and grave Dante weaving well
> His dark-eyed thought into a song divine,
> Drawing high poetry from heaven and hell.   *110361*

Nowhere else does Bridges praise Dante so highly; but are we to aver that he set his memory too hard a task, or did he purposely weld different episodes together? Styx is a marsh (*palude*) not a pit; sinners of wrath are shown on the surface of the mud that 'up-bubbles' because of the slothful spirits sunk beneath it (*Inf.* vi.106–16 and 117–26). Neither are the *accidiosi* particularly unkind to Mirth; and Bridges would rather seem to refer to the hypocrites of *Inf.* xxiii. Did the tone of the dialogue between A. and B. bring about the telescoping of separate episodes of Dante's *Inferno*?

Similar perplexities confront one in the *Testament of Beauty*. The harpies of Bk. I, 217ff. were no doubt suggested by *le brutte arpie* of *Inf.* xiii.9–15, who, however, do not torture the damned spirits by snatching away the dainties put before them as Bridges describes:

> Unlike
> those damn'd souls by the Harpies tantalized in Hell
> whose tortur it was to see their ostentatious feast
> snatch'd from their reach—but he sitting with the dainties
> out-spredd before him would see them, nor ever feel
> any desire nor memory of their old relish.

The poet Laureate was obviously at liberty to describe and to make the harpies act as he chose. By postulating that he had passages of the *Commedia* in his mind one restrains his creative freedom in a way that may possibly be unjustified. The pagan tradition had not placed the harpies in hell; it was Dante who did so; Bridges, supposedly, took over their location from Dante; still, why should not their actions be different? Granting even some foundation to these perplexities, one still feels inclined to think that the 'birthplace' of Bridges' harpies was in Dante's hell: whether he looked up the passage in order to verify their activities and intentionally changed their task, or trusted unduly to his memory, is ultimately irrelevant.

On the contrary the long passage concerned with St. Francis (*Testament of Beauty*, i.239–75) clearly echoes the account of *Purg.* xi. The facts could of course be found in several sources, and no definite verbal contacts are traceable. The general tone, however, compels one to think that Bridges had read and was remembering what Dante wrote.

The use of the words 'Vita Nuova' (*Testament of Beauty*, i.142) is of no real significance, but with the account of the Provençal poets (*Testament of Beauty*, iii.632–740, especially 731–40) one's perplexities are revived. The story in Book III is so compressed as to reach the border of inaccuracy. At a certain point, making a start from the Manichaean heresy, the poet records its revival in Provence, where it was crushed by the crusade against the Albigenses; and then:

> Yet many Troubadours escaping from slaughter
> fled to the Italian cities where the New Learning
> gave kind asylum to their secret flame; and ere
> within the Church's precincts they had raised a song,
> Chivalry had won acceptance in the ideal of sex
> and, blending with the worship of the Mother of God,
> assured the consecration of MARRIAGE, still unknown
> save to the christian folk of Europe whence it sprang.
> Thus, as it came to pass, the second Essene War
> brought the New Life in which full soon Dante was born.

Were it not for the mention of Dante's name at the end, it would be as pedantic to point out historical inaccuracies in so rapid a conspectus as to attempt to prove that it may partly be based on paragraph xxv of the *Vita Nuova*. In fitting distant events together and at times suggesting unexpected connexions between them, Bridges was bound to overlook historical evidence, or rather, to make free with it. 'Was bound' is possibly the wrong expression; 'enjoyed' would describe his feeling better. He was running in his mind through so vast a field that to leap over obstacles became an easier and more natural course than to skirt them.

A reader may also feel challenged by lines 13–14 of Book IV:

> *L'anima vaga delle cose belle*, as saith
> the Florentine. . . .

Whom could Bridges mean by 'the Florentine' but Dante? He never uses this expression to indicate any other citizen of Florence. But Dante never wrote, nor could have written, so drab a line. Mr. Nowell Charles Smith in his *Notes on the Testament of Beauty*[1] pointed out that the source is a madrigal written by Michelangelo, that Bridges translated in a poem beginning:

> My eyes for beauty pine,
> My soul for Goddes grace.[2]

How could Bridges fail to remember this, and how could he refer to Michelangelo simply as 'the Florentine'? Did he attribute to Dante the words of Michelangelo through a slip of memory? Michelangelo's madrigal begins:

> Gli occhi miei vaghi delle cose belle
> E l'alma insieme della sua salute. . . .

In the *Testament of Beauty* the compression of almost two lines into one brings about a rather distressing result. If he remembered that the words, however clumsily refashioned, were Michelangelo's, why did he quote them in Italian? He must have felt that by doing so, in the way he did, he necessarily made Dante responsible for them. It would be absurd to suggest that Bridges had a minute information of the whole of Dante's work. Even when reading he was wilful; he read what he liked best; discarded, disregarded, or forgot the rest. But the personality of Dante Alighieri had impressed him in the years of his youth; and as the poet of the *Growth of Love* was charmed by the *Vita Nuova* at least as early as 1876, the poet of the *Testament of Beauty*—which contained the sum total of his intellectual and human experience, of his dreams and his ideals—who conceived the plan of a poem as serious and thoughtful as any other

---

[1] Oxford University Press, 1940, p. 56.   [2] *Shorter Poems*, iv.9.

that ever was written, could not but turn to 'grave Dante' as he called the Florentine poet.

Bearing in mind the title Bridges had originally chosen for the poem he was composing: *De Hominum Natura*,[1] one may imagine that it was Lucretius who first pointed the way to him, while Milton was his trusted guide, as Virgil was Dante's. Dante had himself great claims to his attention apart from his fame and his craftsmanship. He had intended to *descriver fondo a tutto l'universo* from a strictly orthodox and medieval standpoint, just as Bridges meant to do from the point of view of a modern well-informed intellectual. Furthermore, he was not less proud of being a Man of Kent, a descendant, presumably, of the first Saxons who settled in England,[2] than Dante was of his reputed Roman forefathers. Neither of the two poets took kindly to the conditions of society in his day. Both were conservative by nature and in their political views, and both were devoted to literature and to poetry; each of them acknowledged his master; and Bridges would have gladly accepted the chevaleresque and poetic 'service' of the troubadours, and maybe also the idealization of woman made by the poets of the *Stil nuovo* and by Dante himself. If the verbal echoes are relatively few, and if the reminiscences that can be ascertained are not many, a spiritual parallel—that would of course not imply equality—could be made between Dante and the poet of Chilswell who was certainly not less outspoken than the old Florentine is reported to have been.

---

[1] Edward Thompson, *Robert Bridges* (Oxford University Press, 1944), p. 102.

[2] E. Thompson, op. cit., pp. 1–2.

6

The Symbol of the Gryphon in *Purgatorio* xxix.108 and following Cantos

COLIN HARDIE

IN his *Dante Dictionary* Toynbee accurately says: 'the Griffin in the mystical Procession in the Terrestrial Paradise, commonly understood to be symbolical of Christ; its two-fold nature, half lion, half eagle, representing the two-fold nature of Christ, human and divine'; and he quotes the references in the successive cantos, in which Dante stresses the double nature of the creature, doppia fiera, animal binato, biforme fera, and, above all, the line which is probably responsible for the unanimity of critics, ancient and modern,[1] in interpreting the symbol as of Christ (la fiera), 'Ch'è sola una persona in due nature' (xxxi. 80), since it seems to echo the creeds.

Under the heading 'Processione mistica' Toynbee gives a fuller account of Dante's description:

a griffin, whose wings stretch upward out of sight through the bands of colour ('sette liste', vv. 77, 110); the midmost of which is between the two wings, the others being outside, three on each side (vv. 106–12); the bird part of the griffin is of gold, the lion part of white and vermilion (vv. 113–14).

Later in the same article Toynbee gives his interpretation, 'which is to a certain extent that of Butler', and claims for it that it is 'fairly satisfactory on the whole'. Such an interpretation should be judged as a whole, but I quote only what Toynbee here says of the Gryphon:

the griffin (v. 108) is Christ, the lion part, which is of the colour of flesh (Canto v.10), representing his human nature, the bird part of

---

[1] Most recent is G. B. Ladner, 'Vegetation Symbolism and the Concept of Renaissance' in *de Artibus Opuscula. Essays for Panofsky*, ed. Willard Meiss (N.Y. Univ. Press, 1961), i.303–22: 308 'a griffon symbol of Christ'.

gold (Canto v.11), his divine nature; the division of his seven bands by his wings, so that one band is between them, and three on either side, symbolizes, according to Scartazzini (whose interpretation of this puzzling part of the allegory seems the most plausible), the union of Divinity and Humanity—the three bands on each side are the symbol of the Divinity (as represented by the Trinity), and, if to either of these groups of three be added the middle band, the result is four, the symbol of Humanity, the total making up the mystic number seven, representing the union of Divinity and Humanity, as exemplified in the two-fold nature of Christ.

Toynbee does not discuss the meaning of the passage, *Purg.* xxxi.118–23, to emphasize the importance of which Dante adds one of his addresses to the reader, 124–6.

His references to the Song of Songs deserve to be given in full and indeed expanded: (10) 'Dilectus meus candidus et rubicundus; electus ex millibus'. (11) 'Caput eius aurum optimum. Comae eius sicut elatae palmarum, nigrae quasi corvus.' (12) 'Oculi eius sicut columbae super rivulos aquarum, quae lacte sunt lotae, et resident iuxta fluenta proxima.' To which vi.1 may be added: 'Dilectus meus descendit in hortum suum ad areolam aromatum, ut pascatur in hortis, et lilia colligat' (cf. *Purg.* xxx.21: 'manibus o date lilia plenis').

Toynbee is right in saying that the gryphon is 'commonly understood to be symbolical of Christ', the eagle being taken to represent his divinity, and the lion his humanity. The older commentators, as represented by *La D.C. nella figurazione artistica e nel commento secolare,* ii.679–80 (UTET, Torino, 1931), seem indeed to be unanimous. They state their opinion, and do not argue the point, even to the extent of referring to *Purg.* xxxi.80. The moderns do the same,[1]

---

[1] With one exception, quoted by Toynbee himself in his Addenda, p. 564:
'I am indebted to Professor John Earle (Professor of Anglo-Saxon, 1849–54, 1876–1903) for the following outline of his interpretation of the symbolism of the Griffin in the Terrestrial Paradise: "The Griffin in the D.C. symbolises the general body of the faithful, the bulk of the Christian congregation, the simple and unlearned folk; and this figure is the complement of the figure of Beatrice, which represents the *élite*, the dignity, authority, wisdom and government of the Christian Church. The dual nature of the Griffin represents the dual nature of man, the earthly and spiritual (cf. *Mon.* iii.xvi.75–82), for which the ideal government, in D's theory, is the two-fold monarchy, that of the Emperor for things temporal, and that of the Pope for things eternal." '

occasionally referring to Isidore, *Orig.* xii.2, 17, as Scartazzini-Vandelli and Gmelin do, as if the interpretation of the gryphon as a symbol of Christ is to be found there, which it is not. All that Isidore says is: 'gryphes vocatur, quod sit animal pennatum et quadrupes. Hoc genus ferarum in Hyperboreis nascitur montibus. Omni parte corporis leones sunt; alis et facie aquilis similes; equis vehementer infesti, nam et homines vivos discerpunt.' Isidore seems to derive this from Servius (on Virgil, *Ecl.* viii.27 iungentur cum gryphes equis) who, however, adds one phrase that Isidore omits, after 'equis vehementer infestae', viz. 'Apollini consecratae'. Isidore changes Servius' gender, to agree with masculine 'gryphes', whereas Servius had 'ferarum' in mind.

This information is ultimately derived from Herodotus, (iii.116 and iv.13). Herodotus mentions his source, the epic *Arimaspeia* of Aristeas of Proconnesus, from whom Aeschylus too drew his picture of gryphons in the *Prometheus* 803–6. Herodotus and Aeschylus do not describe the elements that make up the gryphon, since they were familiar from works of art, but Pausanias (1. xxiv.6) describing Pheidias's great chryselephantine statue of Athena in the Parthenon on the Athenian acropolis, mentions the 'grypes'

This explanation is printed more fully in *The Purgatory of Dante Alighieri*, Part II, The Earthly Paradise, translated by C. L. Shadwell, with an introduction by John Earle (Macmillan, London, 1899), pp. ci–cxv.

Earle adds (p. civ): 'The application of these words (*Purg.* xxxii.43–45) is so hopeless that the commentators here have fallen back on the idea that the tree means the Empire, and then they quote the words of Jesus: "Render unto Caesar the things that are Caesar's"—as evidence of His respect for the Roman Empire. But who can be satisfied with such an explanation? Let us only ask ourselves this question: Is it conceivable that Dante could have made prophets and apostles offer to Christ such a speech as this by way of a beatification? It sounds like the parental voice approving a good child that has been at large in a garden and plucked no fruit.'

The Gryphon, then, for Earle, represents plain and simple folk with no 'curiosity' for knowledge (hence *Purg.* xxxii.26–27), and he argues that 'binato' means 'twice-born', which Christ was not, but the regenerate, reborn in Him, are. He further interprets 'il seme d'ogni giusto' as faith, the seed of all justification, comparing *Par.* xii.95–96) and *Purg.* xxxi.46: 'il seme del pianger'.

But Earle has no explanation of the reflection in Beatrice's eyes, and adheres to the procession and chariot as symbol of the Church.

on either side of the helmet, and quotes Aristeas for their fighting the one-eyed Arimaspians in defence of the gold, and adds 'they are animals like lions, but have the feathers and beak of an eagle. So much for gryphons.'

No more need be said on the classical background, in view of J. D. P. Bolton's thorough discussion in *Aristeas of Proconnesus* (Oxford, 1962). He illustrates also the connexion of gryphons with Apollo, in the Hyperborean regions.

Isidore's words, or Servius', are often repeated, e.g. by Hugh of St. Victor, *de bestiis* iii.4 (*P.L.* 177): 'de gryphe. gryphs seu, ut Isidorus scribit, gryphes est animal pennatum . . . nam et homines vivos discerpit, et integros in nidum asportat'. The provenance of the last sentence is not clear. Hugh of St. Victor offers no interpretation; the earliest interpretation of the symbolism known to me is in Rabanus Maurus, *de universo* xxii *libri*: viii.1 *de bestiis*: 'griphes vocatur, quod sit animal pennatum etc.'; he quotes Isidore accurately and without addition, but adds on his own: 'hi possunt significare ferocitatem persecutorum et elationem superborum, qui infesti sunt hominibus qui simplicatatem Christianam sequuntur et rationabiliter vivunt.'

The connexion of gryphons with Apollo reappears in the Vatican Mythographer iii.viii (Apollo).16 (*Scriptores rerum mythicorum latini tres*, ed. G. H. Bode, Cellis, 1834): 'inde etiam tria insignia circa eius (Apollinis) simulacrum videmus, lyram quae nobis harmoniae caelestis imaginem monstrat, gryphen (gryphum, grypheum), qui eum etiam terrenum numen ostendit, sagittas quibus infernus et noxius deus indicatur.' This is very far from any suggestion that the gryphon can symbolize the two Natures in one Person, and indeed the connexion of gryphons with the earth is odd and obscure. But Vat. Myth. ii.18 has it too:

Triplex Apollinis potestas: constat autem triplicis esse Apollinem potestatis, et eundem esse Solem apud Superos, Liberum patrem in terris, Apollinem apud Inferos. unde etiam tria insignia circa eius simulacrum videmus, lyram quae nobis caelestis harmoniae imaginem monstrat; *quadrigam*, quae etiam *terrenum numen* ostendit; sagittas, quibus inferni deus et noxius indicatur, unde et Apollo Grece late perdens dicitur.

Quadrigam is Angelo Mai's reading, but the MSS read 'scribe meum, griphen eum, gripe meum', and Bode would prefer, rightly, to read 'gryphem'.

Much more promising is the suggestion contained in a passage of Claudian, *in* vi *Consul. Hon.* xxviii.30–32:

> At si Phoebus adest et frenis grypha iugalem
> Riphaeo tripodas repetens detorsit ab axe,
> Tunc silvae, tunc antra loqui, tunc vivere fontes,

where a pair of gryphons draw the chariot of the Sun.

Sidonius also has Apollo's chariot drawn by gryphons in *Carm.* xxii: Bacchus, in a chariot drawn by tigers (line 23), approaches Thebes (64), when he sees Apollo approach, 66ff.:

> cum videt Aonia venientem Delion arce.
> grypas et ipse tenet. vultus his laurea curvos
> fronde lupata ligant; hederis quoque circumplexis
> pendula lora virent; sensim fera subvolat ales
> aerias terraeque vias, ne forte citato
> alarum strepitu lignosas frangat habenas.

Bacchus' tigers carry him up into the air, but Sidonius seems to stress that gryphons are adapted both to air and land in the words 'aerias terraeque vias'. ('at ipse' would seem to be better than 'et ipse', and the Loeb translator says 'but', yet leaves et in his text.)

The context of *Purg.* xxix, being largely Biblical in derivation, and having a specific reference to Ezekiel (100) (but note that the classical Argus is mentioned at 95), suggests that the gryphon should be sought in the Bible. But it will scarcely be found there, except in Leviticus xi.13–20, a list of unclean birds not to be eaten, that is repeated in Deuteronomy xiv.12–19. These birds are, of course, real birds, and mostly of identifiable species, eagle, vulture, ostrich, swan, hoopoe, &c. 'Gryphem' occurs in second place after the eagle: 'haec sunt quae de avibus comedere non debetis, et vitanda sunt vobis: aquilam, et gryphem, et haliaeetum, (14) et milvum et vulturem iuxta genus suum, (15) et omne corvini generis in similitudinem suam', &c., and the list ends with the curious addtion: '(20) omne de volucribus quod graditur super quatuor pedes, abominabile erit vobis . . . (23) quidquid autem ex volucribus quatuor tantum habet pedes, execrabile erit vobis.'

Professor G. R. Driver, *Palestine Exploration Fund Quarterly Statement* (1955) 'Birds in the O.T., I. Birds in Law', pp. 5–20, has discussed the γρύψ, which the Septuagint uses to translate Hebrew Peres. The cognate word paras 'smashed' suggests that it may be Arrian's vulture, the 'black vulture' which drops its victim from a great height on to a rock or stone in order to 'smash' its bones (cf. 'ossifrage' in the Authorized Version). (The bird which drops a tortoise on Aeschylus's head and so kills him, meaning to smash the tortoise on him and not him with the tortoise, is, in the *Vita Aeschyli* and *Suda*, called simply an eagle (ἀετός). Perhaps the gryphon disliked Aeschylus because he had made the species the 'hounds of Zeus' instead of Apollo's—Ζηνὸς ἀκραγεῖς κύνας, γῦπας—or took his bald head for a promising stone.)

The Glossa Ordinaria on Lev. xi.13 explains why the eagle is unclean; 'quae vivit de morte et rapina aliarum avium'. Nicolaus de Lyra is quoted for his reference to Ugutio, whose *Magnae derivationes* Dante is known to have made much use of: 'ita quod aliquando equum cum equite rapit, ut dicit Ugutio', and Ugutio, in fact, s.v. griphes, gives the usual information: 'ales pennatus et quadrupes . . . leonibus similes post alas et faciem . . . equos infestant . . . adeo quod equitem armatum cum equo in sublime rapiant et hyperboreis vescantur (nascantur) partibus'. The Glossa also quotes a symbolic interpretation:

quae ad contemplativorum vitam pertinent, adiungit; sicut enim in oblatione sacrificiorum proprium capitulum eis deputavit, sic et in cibis. Verum enim abominandum, quemlibet contemplationi vacantem, sponte tales habere maculas quales in his avibus legislator significat. ait enim aquilam et gryphem &c. . . . per haec raptores et cibum alienum male sectantes et iniustis quaestibus gaudentes figurat. Quaedam ex his rapto vivunt, alia domos penetrant et diripiunt quae reperiunt, his similes sunt qui domos penetrant et captivas ducunt mulierculas peccatis oneratas (1 Tim. iii).

This throws no light on *Purg.* xxix.

On Deut. xiv.12 the Gloss quotes Isidore or Servius: 'et

gryphem quae est quadrupes, capite et alis aquile similis, reliquo corpori leoni, et abundat in Hyperboreis montibus, equis maxime infensa et hominibus'.

Since the gryphon plays no great part in the Bible, it tends to be neglected, e.g. by Epiphanius, *ad Physiologum*, who treats of the lion and the eagle, the pelican, phoenix and peacock, but not the gryphon; by Pseudo-Melito, *Clavis* (Spicilegium solesmense iii, Paris, 1555 (*in quo praecipui veteres auctores de re symbolica proferuntur et illustrantur*). Likewise Vincent of Beauvais, in the *Speculum Naturale*, Liber tricesimus primus (Venice, 1591, vol. i, pp. 409ff.), c. 121: 'de portentis vel monstris fabulosis', explains Geryon '(fuerunt enim tres fratres tante concordie ut in tribus corporibus quasi una anima essent), Sirens (meretrices: naufragium = egestas), gorgons, hydra, scylla', &c., but omits the Gryphon. The Tuscan bestiary in Italian, published by M. S. Garver and K. MacKenzie, *Studi Romanzi* viii (1912), 1–100, 'Il bestiario toscano secondo la lezione dei codici di Parigi e di Londra', includes lion, eagle, Siren, lonza, phoenix, but no gryphon. Migne's Index Allegoricus has nothing either.

Albertus Magnus has a paragraph on the gryphon in his *Libri* xxiii *de animalibus: tractatus unicus de avibus*, c. xxiv, n. 54 (vol. xii (1891), p. 491, of *Collected Works*, ed. Auguste Borgnet), elaborating on whether the forepaws have eagle's or lion's claws (the latter are the more useful kind, since drinking-cups can be made from them), their habitat in the Hyperborean mountains, their enmity to horses and men, and strength 'ut equum ducant et assessorem'. He does not allegorize, but mentions a particular which Cecco d'Ascoli (Francesco Stabili) also mentions in his *Acerba*: 'dicunt autem in montibus illis esse aurum et gemmas et maxime smaragdos; dicunt etiam quod si gryphes in nidis sunt, propter speciale iuvamentum ponunt achates lapides.' In the *Acerba* (ed. Achille Crespi, Ascoli Piceno, 1927) iii, c. 9, Cecco deals with 'remissione die peccati, elezione, nobiltà et fermezza e loro simboli', rondine, calandrio, falcone e grifo', and says of the gryphon:

il grifo assai è forte, ma pur teme
per molti an'mali che son ne li monti . . .   (2465–6)

> sempre nel nido lo smeraldo pone . . .
> per questa pietra fa difensione   (2468–9)

and then draws the moral:

> Così tu devi mettere costei
> dentro nel cuore con la ferma fede
> la qual defende l'uom agli atti rei,
> dall'inimico ch'è il serpente antiquo.   (2471–4)

Crespi refers to Albertus Magnus, vi. 638, notes that a caliph sent a gryphon's claw to Charlemagne in 807—it is in St. Denis and was recognized by Linnaeus as an antelope's horn—and adds 'Dante ne fece il simbolo del Messia (*Purg.* xxxii.26)'.

We have not yet found any support in tradition for this interpretation of Dante's gryphon. I turn from literary sources to visual arts. In *Dictionnaire d'Archéologie chrétienne et de Liturgie* (1924), H. Leclerq, in column 1814, discusses two Christian sarcophagi from Arles, of the seventh century. Between two trees, representing Paradise, two gryphons face each other across a central vase with a spout of water in it. They take the place of the more usual doves, and correspond to Daniel between two lions on the other side of the sarcophagus, and are derived from pagan tombs on which gryphons figure as the guardian of the tomb. Gryphons are common on buckles of dark age barbarian art. Leclerq also mentions a lamp with a handle in the form of a gryphon's head which is surmounted by a cross.

The Spanish *Enciclopedia universal ilustrada* (1925) refers to the gryphon as symbolizing the devil or avarice.

In the *Lexicon für Theologie und Kirche* iv (Freiburg, 1960), coll. 1219–20, s.v. Greif, the derivation from Babylonian Karibu and Hebrew cherub, and the connexion with the chariots of the Sun and of Alexander are mentioned. The gryphon is quoted as a symbol of avarice, and of the union of the two Natures in Christ, for which last the only reference given is *Purg.* 29. The possible connexion with cherub is already noted by Carl Robert in *Pauly-Wissowa, Realencycl.* vii.2, 1902 (1912), who quotes the cherubim guardians of Paradise in Gen. iii.24. (But the word may be Indo-European, from the root found in English grip and grab.) The gryphon as a guardian of churches, flanking portals, is mentioned by V.-H. Debidour, *Le Bestiaire Sculpté du moyen âge en France* (Arthaud, 1961). He observes that gryphons are frequent in pairs as a decorative motif, and are variable in type (as Albertus Magnus also noted, above). But he shows that the gryphon is primarily associated with the ascent to heaven of Alexander the Great. There is no certain example in France (? Le Mans), but Debidour mentions Athens, Urcel, Basel, Fribourg, Remagen, Darmstadt (an Ivory of *c.* 1200), and in Italy the famous mosaic on the floor of Otranto cathedral (1163–6), Fidenza and S. Marco at Venice.

George Cary in his posthumous *The Medieval Alexander* (C.U.P., 1956), discusses Alexander's celestial journey, and illustrates four representations of it (Frontispiece—Otranto; Plate VI—the tapestry in Palazzo Doria, Rome from Tournai, *c.* 1500; Plate IX—Brit. Mus. MS. Royal 20 A. v., fol. 70 verso, north French *c.* 1300: figure 4—a woodcut from the printed *Alexandre le Grant*, Michel Le Noir (Paris, 1506). Cary refers to G. Millet, *Syria* iv (1923), 85–133 'L'Ascension d'Alexandre' as the best study of the ascent, and quotes (n. 53, pp. 296–7) five principal attempts at a symbolic interpretation. They vary, from Alexander as Antichrist to the ascension as a symbol of the Resurrection. Cary quotes (n. 153, p. 346) the disapproval of a German for the pride exemplified by the Ascent.

Cary, however, speaks of God the Father on the Doria tapestry, as in the act of benediction. This seems to be a mistake, since Aby Warburg, *Gesammelte Schriften* i (1932), 'Luftschiff und Tauchboot in der mittelalterlichen Vorstellungswelt', pp. 243–9, speaks of the 'bedenklich abwehrende Geste' of God's *left* hand: Alexander has reached the region of fire (cf. *Purg.* xxvii), the limit for a mortal's journey, and in fear prays to be allowed to return safe to earth, portrayed like a small garden (cf. Dante's aiuola, *Par.* xxii.151). The origin of this journey is in late classical sun-worship; the deified Emperor, a luckier Phaethon, returns to the sun from which he came down. Phaethon is a cherished symbol of Dante's.

The context of *Purg.* xxix.108 shows that in the chariot

of Alexander we come nearest to Dante's associations of thought, since Dante proceeds:

> Non che Roma di carro così bello
> rallegrasse Affricano o vero Augusto,
> ma quel del Sol saria pover con ello;
> Quel del Sol che, sviando, fu combusto &c.
>
> (115–18)

He does not mention Alexander, it is true, but two historical Romans and a mythical Greek, who drove four-horse chariots (cf. *Purg.* xxxii.56–57: 'il sole giunga li suoi corsier'; Virgil, *Aen.* i.568, 'equos Sol iungit'). Dante recurs frequently to Phaethon's unsuccessful attempt to drive the chariot of the Sun (which he knew from Ovid, *Metam.* ii.47–324), in *Inf.* xvii.107: *Purg.* iv.72; *Par.* xxxi.124–6, and also in *Conv.* ii. xiv.5 and in Epistle VIII (Toynbee) XI (S.D.I).4 (the chariot of the Church is led astray, 'non aliter quam falsus auriga Pheton'). Phaethon as a symbol of pride coming to a fall is so deeply engraved on Dante's mind that it obtrudes in *Purg.* xxix, though it is not parallel to the triumphs of Scipio or Augustus, unless, indeed, Phaethon is there to prepare us for the ruin of Beatrice's chariot that is to follow in *Purg.* xxxii. Nor is it surprising that Scipio and Augustus should displace Alexander, and have only one of Alexander's usually four gryphons (two at Otranto) to provide motive power.

For, though Dante praises Alexander for his liberality in *Conv.* iv. xi.14: 'e cui non è ancora nel cuore Alessandro per li suoi reali benefici?' (cf. George Cary, s. v. liberality in index, p. 408) and praises him as the contender for the prize of the universal monarchy who came nearest to achieving it, *Mon.* ii. viii.8: 'maxime omnium ad palmam monarchie propinquus'; it is he rather that Alexander of Pherae whom Dante sees among the tyrants in *Inf.* xii. 107, following Orosius and Lucan in their estimates of his cruelty and having in mind Livy's famous chapters on Alexander, ix.17–19. Dante naturally chooses as the type of triumphator representative of the people who achieved the coveted 'bravium', whom Dante so profoundly admired, the Roman, and though he did not have such a cult of Scipio Africanus as Petrarch (see Aldo S. Bernardo, *Petrarch, Scipio and the 'Africa'*, Baltimore, 1962), he gives him very high honour in *Conv.* IV. v.19; *Mon.* II. x.7; *Inf.* xxxi.115–17; *Par.* xxvii.61–62. As for Augustus, he had the testimony of Virgil, *Aen.* viii.714 above all.

Dante had good reason too for substituting one gryphon for four horses. Beatrice's chariot was to bring her on, not to be driven by her, and on level ground. For this four legs were better than the two talons of an eagle. Yet the eagle was wanted to fly upwards, when the chariot was unyoked and bound to the tree, *Purg.* xxxii.89: 'li altri dopo il grifon sen vanno suso', as it had flown the chariot down from highest heaven to the earthly Paradise.

An explicit reference to the gryphon-chariot (or cage) of Alexander might have carried with it what M. Debidour calls 'tout le saugrenu qu'il comporte', the rather grotesque legs of mutton on the spears which served to attract the gryphons into flight, like the proverbial carrot hung before a donkey. We have seen too that the gryphon carries Apollo's chariot in Claudian, and is called 'Apollini consecratus' by Servius.

We have found nothing in the tradition to suggest the gryphon even distantly as a symbol of Christ, except perhaps the interpretation of Alexander's ascent as a symbol of the Resurrection. This, however, does not imply that Dante could not so use it, if he wished, but it means that in his use of the symbol he had to make his new meaning plain and unmistakable. The commentators, old and modern, have been satisfied of this, without any hesitations and without argument.

In *Purg.* xxix the gryphon, though precisely described, is given no special prominence, and in *Purg.* xxx.1ff., when the Procession halts, the twenty-four elders turn round to face the chariot, and it is to the chariot, and not to the gryphon, that they look 'come a sua pace' (9), and one of them hails Beatrice with the words from the Song of Songs iv.8: 'veni de Libano, sponsa mea; veni de Libano, veni', implying that Beatrice here stands for the Church, the Bride of Christ. The salutation is taken up by the whole company, but in the curious form, *Benedictus qui venis,* curious that is, if the words are addressed to Beatrice, and not to the gryphon, as many commentators assume. The words are, of course, those which saluted Christ when he entered Jerusalem on Palm Sunday, Mat. xxi.9 (derived from Psalm 117–26), but if they are transferred to Beatrice as, for instance, Gmelin says, we should expect the feminine *Benedicta quae venis*, which Porena puts in his text (except that he does not alter 'qui' to 'quae'!), on the model of *Purg.* xxix.85-87.

> Benedicta tue
> ne le figlie d'Adamo, e benedette
> sieno in eterno le bellezze tue.

Interest is concentrated on Beatrice, and the gryphon goes unmentioned, until *Purg.* xxxi.79—81:

> e le mie luci, ancor poco sicure,
> vider Beatrice volta in su la fera
> ch'è sola una persona in due nature.

This does indeed seem, at first sight at least, to be a Christological formulation. But in *Inf.* xii.83–84, Dante describes another double beast, the centaur Chiron, and the point, the chest, where the two natures meet

> che già li era al petto
> dove le due nature son consorti.

Chiron is not called 'a person', but he more clearly is one than the gryphon, who utters one line only, *Purg.* xxxii.48. In *Purg.* xxxi.113 the four ladies lead Dante

> al petto del grifon . . .
> ove Beatrice stava volta a noi,

so that he stands by the gryphon, as before Virgil stood by the Centaur, al petto. The two natures of the Centaur are man and beast; could the gryphon not likewise symbolize the union in man of an animal nature, the lion, as in *Inf.* i, with a spiritual nature (of perception, intuition, and reason) in the eagle? In the gryphon the two natures are harmoniously blended, so that it loses no feathers, *Purg.* xxxii.27: 's'ì che, però, nulla penna crollonne', unlike the eagle which loses its feathers at *Purg.* xxxii.126 as it strikes downwards at the tree. The proper function of the eagle is to look upwards into the sun, *Par.* i.48; xx.32.

The pointed contrast between losing no feather and losing many or all shows that Dante associated the aquiline part of the gryphon with the separate and independent eagle that strikes the tree and chariot. This surely implies that the eagle's feathers and the eagle must have the same meaning in both places. The eagle that loses its feathers is clearly not divine in the sense of sinless, since its repeats the sin of Adam.

If, then, Dante is to establish his new and untraditional symbolism of the gryphon, he ought surely to make the eagle in the immediate context have the same meaning as in the gryphon. There is no lion in the immediate context, but no reader could have forgotten the lion of *Inf.* i.45, which is indeed the only symbolic lion in the *Comedy* (the lions of *Inf.* xxxi.118 and *Purg.* vi.66 are literal; those of *Inf.* xvii. 60; xxvii.50; *Par.* xii.54 are heraldic; the constellation is mentioned in *Par.* xvi.37 and xxi.14; in *Inf.* xxx.8 Athamas in his madness imagines his wife and children to be lioness and cubs); except for the passing reference in *Par.* vi.107–8, where eagle and lion are at enmity, as they should not be if the insubordinate lion, Charles II of Naples, were to submit to the eagle, the Empire. The lion in *Inf.* i is accepted as a symbol of pride that is one form of corruption in human nature, and the same kind of meaning appears in *Inf.* xxvii. 75, where Guido da Montefeltro describes his acts as 'non . . . leonine, ma di volpe'.

The lion then does not symbolize human nature as such in contrast to divine, but one aspect of (corrupt) human nature; and if we look elsewhere in Dante for lions, we find *Ep.* v.4 a lion that is a symbol of Christ as divine Saviour, the 'leo fortis de tribu Iuda, radix David' quoted from Apoc. v.5. The eagle of *Purg.* xxxii.112 is generally assumed to be the imperial eagle, the symbol of the Roman Empire, as in *Par.* vi. (and in passing, at *Purg.* x.80) but in the *Comedy* before *Purg.* xxxii. is reached, eagles are by no means always imperial, nor always divine. The first eagle of the *Comedy* is the poet, Homer, in *Inf.* iv.96; and the eagle in

Purg. ix.20 turns out to be the disguise assumed in Dante's dream by St. Lucy, a symbol of grace. The eagle of justice in the Sixth Heaven, *Par*. xviii.107, is surely not the symbol of imperial justice, but of God's justice in His inscrutable providence, and the Emperors Constantine and Trajan are in its eye, *Par*. xx.31–32, not as emperors, but as souls saved by grace, *Par*. xx.71. In *Par*. xxvi.53 the 'aquila di Cristo' is not Christ himself, but St. John the Evangelist, and in this extremely familiar symbolism of the four evangelists the lion is, of course, the symbol of St. Mark. In *Ovide Moralisé* (ed. de Boer 1915) ii.759–71, the four-horsed chariot of the Sun becomes the chariot of God, drawn by the four evangelists.

In all this there is nothing to suggest, still less establish, the symbolic meaning of the gryphon as the union of perfect human nature with divine. The gryphon of *Purg*. xxix is indeed faultless in obedience, and an agent of the divine grace that restores the blasted tree. But as a symbol of the mystery of the incarnation it seems crude and unbefitting. In *Par*. xxx in the final vision Dante expresses the mystery of the Second Person of the Trinity by saying that the second of the three rings (116), reflecting the first 'come iri da iri' (118), somehow

> dentro da se, del suo colore stesso,
>   mi parve pinta de la nostra effige,
>   per che il mio viso in lei tutto era messo.   (130–2)

But a gryphon is the union of two natural species in a quite external manner which produces a monster, a contradiction of nature: it is not the union of an uncreated nature (in a different sense, an analogical sense, of this word) with a created nature that it permeates, unites 'hypostatically' with, so that the human form remains visibly the same, as in the Transfiguration which Dante recalls at *Purg*. xxxii. 73ff. It is difficult to believe that Dante could have chosen a monster (of the same kind as a centaur or as Geryon) as a symbol of Christ, especially when there was nothing in tradition to support his choice. A man with three faces was in Dante's time a possible symbol of the Trinity, though more usually a symbol of the Devil; but Dante uses it for

Satan in *Inf.* xxxiv, because it is monstrous. Much later, in 1445, Sant' Antonino, as bishop of Florence, denounced 'unam personam cum tribus capitibus' as an image of the Trinity, 'quod monstrum est in rerum natura' (quoted by G. J. Hoogewerff, *Atti della Ponteficia Acc. romana di archeologia*, Ser. iii, Rendiconti xix (1942–3; published 1944): ' "Vultus Trifrons": emblema diabolico, immagine irreproba della SS. Trinità, pp. 205–45). Hoogewerff notes that only in 1628 did Pope Urban VIII formally condemn the 'vultus trifrons' as a symbol of the Trinity, and that in origin it is a very old symbol of solar deity, e.g. Lug in Gaul identified with Mercury and Apollo by the Romans; we have seen in *Vat. Myth.* II. 18 that the solar Apollo is triple.

The *Codex Iuris Canonici*, promulgated by Benedict XI in 1917 (Città del Vaticano, 1930), p. 434, Can. 1279, par. 1, reads: 'nemini licet in ecclesiis . . . ullam insolitam ponere . . . imaginem', and in par. 3: 'nunquam sinat Ordinarius in ecclesiis aliisve locis sacris exhiberi falsi dogmatis imagines vel quae debitam decentiam et honestatem non praeseferant, aut rudibus periculosi erroris occasionem praebeant.' These canons go back only to the Council of Trent, session XXV, but Dante's symbol is 'insolita', and in its juxtaposition of two created natures perhaps 'occasio erroris'.

Dante says that the part of the gryphon that is eagle is of the colour of gold. But this does not prove the eagle to be divine, but precious and regal. As the possession of reason is what distinguishes man from the beasts and makes him the image of God, the golden colour could indicate the value of the rational soul and its power to rule the lower souls.

The acceptance of the Gryphon in Dante as a symbol of Christ by the commentators seems to be due to hasty assumptions rather than to an examination of the evidence, and, above all, to the presupposition that Beatrice in the chariot with her *cortège* represents the Church and that the Church without its Founder is absurd. But I have already elsewhere expressed my doubts about this presupposition (*DDJ* xxxix (1961), 137–72, 'Beatrice's chariot in the Earthly Paradise'), and about the usual interpretations of the eagle that strikes the tree and the chariot.

There are, however, further arguments to be considered. First one point and then the crucial question about what Dante sees reflected in Beatrice's eyes.

First, when the gryphon shed no feather at *Purg*. xxxii.27, it is in contrast with the eagle of 126. But in 43ff, when the company exclaims

> beato sei, grifon, che non discindi
> col becco d'esto legno,

it contrasts the gryphon with Adam (37), who despoiled the plant of its leaves and whose sinful successor despoils it a second time (*Purg*. xxxiii.57: or due volte dirubata) after its restoration (59: s'innovò) from contact with the chariot. The gryphon would thus seem to be the second Adam, Christ. In reply the gryphon makes its only utterance:

> sì si conserva il seme d'ogni giusto,

which, the commentators (e.g. Scartazzini-Vandelli) say, is a paraphrase of the words of Christ to St. John the Baptist in Mat. iii.15: 'sic enim decet nos implere omnem iustitiam'; though the resemblance is very far from close, indeed exists only in the relationships sic—sì and giusto—iustitia. Gmelin protests against the interpretation, but has nothing to put in its place. The meaning of the tree is much disputed; for many it represents the Empire, like the eagle which despoils it. Porena is a good example of the difficulties which the usual public interpretation involves. For the phrase 'arbore robusto' Gmelin quotes arbor robusta in Daniel iv.17 'which in Nebuchadnezzar's dream means the Babylonian Kingdom': but in verse 19 Daniel explains which Nebuchadnezzar himself is the tree, and Dante's 'seme' would seem to be derived from verses 12, 20, 23: 'verumtamen *germen* radicum eius (arboris) in terra sinite'; 20: 'attamen germen radicum eius in terra dimittite'; 23: 'quod autem praecepit ut relinquetur germen radicum eius . . . regnum tuum tibi manebit, postquam cognoveris potestatem esse caelestem'. Then the gryphon ties the chariot to the tree (whatever 'quel di lei a lei lasciò legato' means), symbolizing the union of Church and Empire, the divine and the human, and so externalizing what exists in himself, the union of the two natures, according to Scartazzini-Vandelli.

The renovation of the tree is accompanied by a hymn, which Dante cannot understand (61): 'io non l'intesi', and yet is rapt into ecstasy. He compares himself to the apostles at the Transfiguration who were overwhelmed by the Glory and woke again, at Christ's words, to see Him as He had been before the Transfiguration (81):

> ed al maestro suo cangiata stola.

When Dante wakes, he is told that the Gryphon has ascended, with the rest following

> con più dolce canzone e più profonda.

When *Par.* xiv is reached with Dante's vision of the Cross and of Christ, we cannot but see in this passage of *Purg.* xxix an anticipation of the fuller and more explicit development of his ecstasy. The phrase 'io non lo intesi' occurs again only in the further development in *Par.* xv.39 where Cacciaguida speaks even more 'profondo' (but cf. xiv.120 and 126).

Now in my opinion Caccioguida here foreshadows the final vision which will be accorded to Dante in *Par.* xxxiii. This suggests that Dante's ecstasy in *Purg.* xxxiii, described in similar terms, has a similar personal cause, peculiar to him—namely, that the foundation of his being, 'il fondamento che natura pone', his vegetative soul, is restored, as is appropriate in the Earthly Paradise. Only on that restored foundation can the animal and rational souls be in their turn restored, and so 'conditioned' for the final vision in the Celestial Paradise.

Finally, we come to the reflection of the gryphon in Beatrice's eyes. The whole passage from *Purg.* xxxi.115 to the end of the canto, including the difficult penultimate line, 144: 'là dove armonizzando il ciel t'adombra', is crucial, but especially the tercets in which Dante draws the reader's attention to an astonishing phenomenon: 'pensa, lettor, se io mi maravigliava'.

The four ladies call Beatrice's eyes, which are her 'prima bellezza' (in contrast to 'la seconda' (138), which is her smile), 'li smeraldi' (associated, as we have seen, with gryphons by Cecco d'Ascoli)

> ond' Amor già ti trasse le sue armi,

in allusion to the 'stilnovistic' theory of love generated by and in the eyes (Sonnet in *Vita Nuova* 21; Canzone *Donne ch'avete*; *Rime* LXV, and in the *Com.*, *Par.* xxvi.14; xxviii.12). But in the period of the *Vita Nuova* the light of Beatrice's eyes is her own, with no suggestion of a reflection. Here Beatrice gazes steadily with her eyes, 'che pur sopra il grifone stavan saldi' (120), at the gryphon, and has to be adjured by the attendant ladies to turn her eyes on her devotee:

> Volgi, Beatrice, volgi li occhi santi
> ... al tuo fedele.   (133–4)

She is, one supposes, absorbed in the beatific vision, if the gryphon is a symbol of Christ. The reflection of the gryphon in her eyes is then compared to the reflection of the sun in a mirror, for which the commentators quote Ovid, *Metam.* iv.346ff., where the nymph Salmacis sees Hermaphroditus strip to bathe.

> Tum vero stupuit, nudaeque cupidine formae
> Salmacis exarsit. flagrant quoque lumina nymphae,
> non aliter quam cum puro nitidissimus orbe
> opposita speculi referitur imagine Phoebus.

The idea of the flickering and changing image of the sun perhaps comes from Virgil, *Aen.* viii.22–25 (the tremulum ... lumen, to which Aeneas's changing thoughts are compared). The gryphon, like the sun, remains unaltered, but its image changes, and Benvenuto da Imola comments: 'et est propriissima comparatio de sole ad Christum qui ut sol iustitiae [est], et de oculis Beatricis ad speculum, quia oculus est de natura speculi'; and he then speaks of 'diversis operationibus, quia nunc humanis nunc divinis vel nunc literaliter vel nunc figuraliter'.

The *Ottimo* will serve as an example of what the commentators say: 'cioè che Cristo per un modo, in quanto ha seco vera umanitade si mostra nelle dimostrazioni di

Teologia per un modo, e per altro modo si dimostra in quanto
è Iddio.' Some, however, show a little uneasiness that there
are two natures reflected not in two, but many changing
images, or perhaps in two sets of images:

> or con gli uni or con gli altri reggimenti   (123)

cf. Landino: 'Le Sacre Lettere non pongono sempre
Cristo una medesima cosa, ma mutante in varie figure'; or
Vellutello: 'perchè non sempre la Scrittura Sacra figura
Cristo in umana forma, ma in diverse e più altre'. The
divinity of Christ without His humanity can scarcely be
represented by any figure, but there are forms other than
human, in the Lamb, Lion of Judah, &c. Cesareo finds the
changing image of the unchanged natures to be due to the
incapacity of the human mind to understand their union:
'nella mente del comprensore, figurata in Beatrice, si con-
vengono considerare l'una appo l'altra, con gli atti di
ciasceduna.' But Gmelin takes a different view: 'dass
Beatrices Augen die beiden Naturen (die göttliche und die
menschliche) abwechselnd spiegeln können, deutet auf ihre
besondere Gabe der Enthüllung göttlicher Wahrheit.' To
decide whether Beatrice is a perfect or imperfect mediatrix
of the divine vision to Dante requires, I suggest, the discussion of a parallel passage in *Par.* xxxiii.113–14, which no
commentator adduces, except that Tommaseo (and others,
Scartazzini-Vandelli, Sapegno) mentions *Purg.* xxxi.121–6
in commenting on *Par.* xxxiii.113–14.

Porena limits the application of the simile of the sun in
the mirror:

la similitudine del Sole e dello specchio è limitata alla reflessione per-
fetta dell' imagine, e non si estende all'oscillazione fra due aspetti,
che nel caso del Sole e dello specchio non ha luogo se pure alcuni
interpreti vogliono vedercela. Quanto al senso allegorico, la teologia
mostra Cristo ora nella sua natura umana, ora nella sua natura divina.

If the sun is reflected in water, as in Virgil's image, its
image shimmers, but Ovid emphasizes the sharp outline of
the reflection in a metal mirror, 'puro nitidissimus orbe',
even if it is dazzling.

The parallel passage in *Par.* xxxiii.109–20 describes

Iced

Dante's own vision of the divine essence, when he has no further need of Beatrice's mediation and she has turned from him to the beatific vision, *Par.* xxxi.93:

> poi si tornò a l'eterna fontana.

Dante rises to the contemplation of three persons in one substance, including the two natures in one of the persons. Within the unity there is reflection: 'e l'un da l'altro come iri da iri/parea riflesso.' The appearance of the unchanging unity changed to Dante, because he was changing under its influence and having his power of sight again raised to a new height as the culmination of the long series of 'conditionings', *Par.* xiv.48, to new intensities of brilliance (e.g. *Par.* i.49–54):

> ma per la vista che s'avvalorava
> in me guardando, una sola parvenza,
> mutandomi io, a me si travagliava.[1]

There is, of course, a great difference in *Par.* xxxiii: Dante can perceive nothing of the reality behind the appearance except what the appearance shows him, whereas in *Purg.* xxxi the gryphon stands firm in front of him and he sees its changing reflection. He can, however, know, by revelation and reason, that the ultimate reality in *Par.* xxxiii is one and unchangeable. The parallel suggests that in *Purg.* xxix.29 Beatrice's eyes should reflect an unchanging divine being, if the usual interpretation were correct.

When, then, Dante sees the gryphon, he sees as one and unchanging what he ought to see as Beatrice sees it, as many and changing (since her vision is pure and his is still very

---

[1] Scartazzini-Vandelli comments: 'si travagliava: si mutava'; and cites Tommaseo: 'travagliatori chiamavansi i prestigiatori': Porena: 'travagliarsi significa propriamente agitarsi: e quindi, detto di una forma, mutarsi continuamente', and he paraphrases 'una parvenza unica mi si rimutava nella mia visione'; and Gmelin: 'sie arbeitete gleichsam in mir'. These expressions seem hardly strong enough, and perhaps 'a me' means more than 'in me' or 'in my sight'. In *Purg.* xxi.1–4 Dante says his thirst for ultimate truth 'mi travagliava'. In French the word has come to mean simply to work, but the English travail retains more of the original idea of torture on three stakes, tripalium: is it not something like 'the vision strove to impose itself on me', 'broke down the barriers of multiplicity in me until there was nothing between me and the Trinity in Unity'?

imperfect); in the final vision he sees the object as many
and changing, not because there is multiplicity and change
in it, but because there is multiplicity and change in him.
When the object has subdued his multiplicity, he can see it
as one in three. In *Par.* xxx.76–80, likewise, what Dante
sees is due to his defective vision:

> il fiume e li topazii . . .
> . . . son di loro vero umbriferi prefazii.
> Non chè da sè sian queste cose acerbe;
> ma è difetto da la parte tua.

If the gryphon is a symbol of Dante's own nature restored,
i.e. of his two 'Souls', animal and spiritual, in close harmony,
then Beatrice is right to see a multiplicity in it that Dante
cannot yet see but will eventually also become aware of as
something to be overcome before he can see the ultimate
unity. Beatrice should not see as multiple and changing a
symbol of Christ (who is the same now and for ever) which
Dante can see as stable.

When Dante sees the one in three and within it the two
natures of Christ in one person, then this multiplicity is
reduced to harmony; his will is in perfect accord with God's
will for him, and he can return from heaven to earth, from
the vision to the task of writing the poem that describes his
journey to the vision.

Moreover, the gryphon, a harmonization of two out of
the three 'Souls' of Dante, proceeds to restore the third,
vegetative, soul (the tree, which the eagle, misdirected
spirit, isolated from the animal soul) by linking it to the
chariot, the symbol of supernatural grace (or, for Dante the
poet, of his inspired poetry).

Now, in gazing at Beatrice's eyes Dante's soul tastes

> quel cibo
> che, saziando di sè, di sè asseta.   (128–9)

This food corresponds to the drink,

> l'acqua onde la femminetta
> Sammaritana dimandò la grazia

of *Purg.* xxi.1–3, and it satisfies 'la sete natural che mai non
sazia' otherwise;

> la concreta e perpetua sete
> del deiforme regno

of *Par*. ii.19–20.

The point of 'saziando . . . asseta' is made again in *Par*. xv.64–66:

> il sacro amore in che io veglio
> con perpetua vista e che m'asseta
> di dolce disiar.

This seems to suggest that what satisfies Dante in Beatrice's eyes is the reflection of deity, Christ's two natures, in them. But Dante's sharp prod of the reader: 'pensa, lettor' (xxxi.124), is designed to alert us to question the meaning of the reflection in Beatrice's eyes, and to wait for further evidence. The thirst is in *Purg*. xxxii.1 'la decenne sete', and the attendants comment on Dante's mode of slaking it ('disbramarsi'): 'troppo fisso' (9). It is not merely that his eyes are dazzled as if by the sun (11), but, as appears later, he is to be weaned from a kind of idolatry of Beatrice. In the fifth heaven, of Mars, he sees the Cross

> il venerabil segno
> che fan giunture di quadranti in tondo

(*Par*. xiv.101–2) and 'in quella croce lampeggiava Christo'. Dante is rapt into ecstasy by the music of the spirits, in whose hymn of praise he gets only 'thou risest again and conquerest'. He then pauses to accuse and excuse himself (without any allusion to the gryphon or the two natures) for having found a rapture sweeter than the delight of Beatrice's eyes,

> proponendo il piacer de li occhi belli
> nei qual mirando mio disio ha posa.

In *Purg*. xix.24 a 'donna santa e presta' (for me certainly to be identified with Beatrice) exposes the sham claim of the siren to give complete satisfaction: 'sì tutto l'appago', and in *Purg*. xxix Beatrice seems to be able to satisfy all Dante's desires.

But in *Par*. xv, too, Dante mentions a second source of paradisiacal rapture other than Beatrice. As in the previous canto the rapture is beyond his full understanding (cf. *Par.* xv.39: 'che io non lo intesi', with *Par.* xiv.120: 'a tal da cui la nota non è intesa' and 126: (come a colui che non intende ed ode'), and it comes this time from the smile in the eyes of Cacciaguida, so that Dante stands between him and Beatrice, stupefatto:

> onde io m'attesi a lui;
> poscia rivolsi a la mia donna il viso,
> e quinci e quindi stupefatto fui;

and he explains why:

> che dentro a li occhi suoi ardea un viso
> tal, ch'io pensai coi miei toccar lo fondo
> de la mia grazia e del mio *paradiso.*

Dante's lack of understanding was inevitable since Cacciaguida's concetto

> al segno dei mortal si soprapose   (42).

This implies that the Paradise which Beatrice offers is intelligible and 'mortal', i.e. natural, due to a restoration of nature, and not '*super*infusa gratia' (28–29).

The theme recurs in *Par.* xviii. and the contrast is resolved by Beatrice herself. Cacciaguida is described as a 'specchio beato' and his message (verbo) to Dante tempers 'col dolce l'acerbo' (3). Then Beatrice comforts him and he turns to her:

> e qual io allor vidi
> ne li occhi santi amore, qui l'abbandono.

All he can say is that, as he gazed on her

> lo mio affetto
> libero fu da ogni altro disire   (14–15)

but he explains further

> fin che (so long as) il piacere eterno, che diretto
> raggiava in Beatrice, dal bel viso
> mi contentava col secondo aspetto,

where 'secondo' means reflected, mediated, indirect (cf. *Par.* i.49).

Just at this point, when Beatrice overwhelms him with the light of her smile, she adds, 'turn away from me to Cacciaguida again': 'volgiti ed ascolta':

> chè non pur nei miei occhi è Paradiso:

Paradise is not only in my eyes.

Later again she diverts him from herself,

> perchè la faccia mia sì t'innamora
> che tu non ti rivolgi al bel giardino
> che sotto i raggi di Cristo s'infiora?
> *(Par.* xxiii.70–72)

But even now we have not done with Beatrice as Paradise and as mirror; the theme culminates in *Par.* xxviii.1–16. Dante gazes at Beatrice's eyes

> nei belli occhi
> onde a pigliarmi fece Amor la corda   (11–12)

and she is 'quella che imparadisa la mia mente' (3).

Two tercets elaborate the simile of the candle seen in a mirror (4–9), and Dante turns from Beatrice to see directly what is reflected in her eyes, and sees 'un punto' (16) (also 41, 95, 101; xxix.12: the point looks back to *Vita Nuova* xii. 4, and forward to *Par.* xxxiii.94). Dante does now without prompting what earlier he had done at her bidding. When the point fades away, *Par.* xxx.113, he turns again to Beatrice and tries for the last time to express her beauty in seven tercets, 16–36. When he has gazed on 'la forma general del paradiso', *Par.* xxxi.52, he turns expecting to find Beatrice as usual at his side, but he has gone. 'Ella ove è?' he exclaims to St. Bernard who replies:

> a terminar lo tuo disiro
> mosse Beatrice me del loco mio.

Beatrice guides him to St. Bernard and intercedes for him, but she is not the final mediator of the vision, and in his last words to her he addresses her as an equal, substituting 'tu' for 'voi'.

All this development of the theme of Beatrice's beauty, her eyes and her smile, and of her as a mirror of God's glory and as guide and mediatrix, who is nevertheless at the last displaced by the 'santo sene', is thus relevant to our question what the gryphon means.

If Dante has to be weaned from his idolatry of Beatrice, then what he sees in her eyes cannot be a symbol of Christ; for he has to by-pass her, precisely in order to see the divine essence.

The address to the reader in *Purg.* xxix draws attention to a problem of great complexity, which is not resolved until Dante sees for himself a multiplicity hiding a unity, as he had before seen in the mirror of Beatrice's eyes multiple images of an apparently stable union of two natures.

But the evidence is not without ambiguity. In *Par.* xiv. where Christ Himself 'lampeggia in quella croce, balena in quell'albor', we should expect some reference to the gryphon, or some hint about the two natures in one person but we get nothing.

Further, Beatrice enjoys the beatific vision at all times, even if she can see Dante in God and seem to give him her full attention. There can be no defect in her apprehension of the union of the two natures in the gryphon; the defect must be in Dante, just as in *Par.* xxxiii his own multiplicity hides the unity and has to be overcome by the working of that unity on him. But in *Purg.* xxix Beatrice surely sees the meaning of the gryphon as Dante cannot yet see it; she sees change and multiplicity where he sees simply the 'doppia fera', 'animal binato', &c.

It is perhaps worth suggesting that there are multiple possibilities in a man's double nature (animal and rational: lion and eagle), but God intends and wills the *one* best achievement of these potentialities. This requires *sacrifice* of all the others; and it is a sacrifice of the greatest gift of God to man, freedom of the will (*Par.* v.22). A vow (ibid. 26) is such a sacrifice, and must be accepted by God (27). I suggest that Dante has in mind here the promise at the end of *Vita Nuova* XLII of a great poem for Beatrice. His failure to keep it is Beatrice's reproach in *Purg.* xxx.103-45. But in *Par.* xiv.93 he makes the sacrifice, which is a precondition of the grace of the final vision. The final vision unifies the multiplicity, and itself is the precondition of the poem, which (for me) is to be the work of the 515, Dante's redeemed self.

I find this divergence between what Dante sees directly and what he sees in Beatrice's eyes easier to accept if the gryphon stands for Dante's restored nature in its two sides, animal and spiritual—redeemed by grace, and therefore necessarily in many respects like the Redeemer, rather than for Christ Himself. At least we cannot be meant to jump to the interpretation of the gryphon as Christ as to something obvious and simple. The interpretation emerges—or does not emerge—in the course of a complex development which ends only with the end of the poem. We are meant to wonder, as Dante wonders—'pensa, lettor, se io mi maravigliava' (*Purg.* xxxi.124), and to look for evidence. The evidence is distorted, if it is simply assumed that the Procession is the Church, and the transformations of the chariot symbolize its history, that Beatrice is a symbol of theology, and that the 515, the heir of the eagle, is an Emperor and Cacciaguida's promised hero Cangrande della Scala.[1] The particular development that I have tried to trace in this paper at least suggests that Beatrice cannot symbolize theology if the mystery of the Resurrection in *Par.* xiv distracts Dante from Beatrice, and if he has two sources of ecstasy, Beatrice and what culminates in the Beatific Vision when Dante has been 'conditioned' by Beatrice to do without her and to go beyond her. She is 'quella donna ch'a Dio mi menava' (*Par.* xviii.4); she guides towards the higher experience, but she does not mediate it, making way for the deeper 'archetype' of the wise old man, the father embodied in the series of figures from Cacciaguida to St. Bernard. Beatrice enlightens Dante about his own personal errors; the general doctrines of theology are discussed in the presence of St. Thomas, St. Peter, St. John.

The primary meaning of the gryphon, before Dante put it in his own new context, is that of a guardian of treasure (of a tomb or of a church or, as the legs of a chair, of the enthroned person) and a winged courser of the Chariot of the Sun or of Alexander the Great, and it often has a

[1] See my article, 'Cacciaguida's Prophecy in Paradiso 17' in *Traditio* xix.267–94 (1963).

negative aspect, as avaricious or devilish, hostile to mankind.

In Dante the gryphon draws Beatrice's chariot, but also acts independently in restoring the tree. As the source of motion could it not represent the animal soul in man, the emotional endowment of will and desire without which 'the intellect moves nothing' as Aristotle said? It links the unmoving tree, vegetative nature, to the chariot, which is a work of reason and of art, not of nature. When the tree is again despoiled and the chariot wrecked, what will restore the tree a second time but the gryphon which restored it before? As in part eagle, it can be the 'heir of the eagle'.

The gryphon is potentially human, as it can speak; on its return it can be expected to be fully human, as the 'messo di Dio'. In *Purg.* ix Dante can see St. Lucy only as an eagle, but in *Par.* xxxii.137 he sees her as she really is, in human form. The beginning of this process of a second restoration seems to me to be the end of *Purgatorio*, xxxiii.143–4, where Dante is baptized and emerges

> sì come piante novelle
> rinovellate di novella fronda

where the word 'new' is repeated three times (cf. *Par.* i.74 'novellamente', and *Purg.* xxx.118–20 for the image of the plant applied to Dante personally). But an interpretation of this sort is inconceivable unless in the *Comedy* Dante revised the notion, that he accepted in the *Convivio* from the neoplatonic tradition, of the radical hostility of body and soul. It is, however, generally assumed that there are only minor differences between the *Convivio* and the *Comedy*. For me the *Comedy* is evidence of a radical revision, indeed a revolution in Dante's thought.

No longer is it the task of the rational soul to keep itself uncontaminated by bodily passions. The corruption of the spirit cannot be set right without restoring the vegetative and animal 'souls' which it has infected, but on which it depends, and with which it must be linked again in harmony. Redemption does not descend from heaven to liberate the rational soul from its material embodiment; it comes up from under foot, from the antipodes, through matter and the body, through the vegetative and animals 'souls' to the rational soul or spirit. Or, to express it otherwise, Dante must go down past the densest and most material centre of the earth (where the being, created most spiritual, Lucifer, is found to be lodged) to find the restoration of his vegetative and animal 'Souls'. Dante's new symbolism must be considered as a whole, in the light of his new attitude. In *Tre donne* he puts the Earthly Paradise at the source of the Nile on this side of the Equator, accessible without going underground through the earth. The symbol of the sunlit hill of *Inf.* i.13 or 'bel monte' of *Inf.* ii.120 needs to be looked at again, and seen, I believe, as the symbol of earthly happiness which Dante has described in *Mon.* iii. xvi and now in the *Comedy* sees to be a delusion. The 'bel monte' is not an anticipation of the Mountain of Purgatory, as is sometimes said. It follows that Virgil is not a symbol of Reason (whether assisted by Grace or not) but a poet whose supernatural knowledge of the other world, shown in his poems and deepened by his experience after death, qualifies him to be a guide in regions unknown to Aristotle. Virgil's knowledge does not only go beyond reason; it falls short of what Aristotle achieved, when in *Purg.* iii Virgil cannot understand Aristotle's doctrine of the relation of body and soul and in *Purg.* xxv makes way for Statius' exposition of it. The 'bel monte' cannot be discussed fully here, still less Virgil. But, anyhow, Dante, in the neoplatonic hostility to the body of the *Convivio*, there (iii. iv.10), denies the possibility of the vision of God's essence in this life, which he makes the goal and climax of the *Comedy*.

In the *Comedy* he constantly insists on his bodily presence, and in *Purg.* xxv develops a new theory of the 'ombre'. He makes the shades long for the restoration of their bodies to them, *Par.* xiv.63. It is within this new framework of ideas that I see the symbolism of the *Comedy*, and the gryphon as an important part of it.

Postscripts

(i) The passage in *Par.* ii.37–45 is to be noted because it expresses a very different conception of the union of the two natures in Christ from that implied by the image of the gryphon. In the gryphon 'one dimension does not admit of a second', nor does 'one body interpenetrate another'. If Dante had meant to symbolize the two natures of Christ in the gryphon, he could scarcely have so soon after written lines 37–45, incompatible with his symbol and without reference to it.

(ii) I note with pleasure that Alan Gilbert, *Dante and His Comedy*, New York U.P. (1963), rejects the traditional interpretation of the gryphon: p. 119, n.2, 'griffin . . . thrice called a *fiera*' (*Purg.* xxxi.80 and 122; xxxii.47), and once an *animale* (xxxii.96) '. . . there are no mythical animals in heaven'; p. 122, 'What is the symbolism of the griffin?'; p. 124, 'In representing divinity he concedes to human weakness as little as he can. Is it likely that he abandons such a practice to typify the Second Person of the Trinity as a mythological draft animal? But the poet is in the reader's hands; each may interpret the allegory as he will.'

(iii) Leone Tondelli, *Il libro delle figure dell' abate Gioachino Da Fiore*. I² S.E.I. Turin (1953). V. 3, pp. 283–5, 'Il grifone che trae il carro trionfale', notes that Dante's representation of Christ as a gryphon is strange and new, but he accepts this interpretation, supposing that Dante derived the symbol from Joachim by combining two of the four beasts, as figured in Plate XV (from the Reggio Codex) of Ezekiel's chariot—namely, the lion and the eagle. He quotes Joachim's comments: Christus resurgendo factus est leo; Christus homo ascendendo in coelum aquila factus est.

But it is a very different thing to fuse two beasts out of four into one, and to link the Resurrection and the Ascension. Why should the lion as resurrection stand for human nature, and the eagle, Christus *homo*, as ascension, stand for the Divine Nature? The resurrection and the ascension are both divine.

Dante had no need of Joachim's figure to envisage either Ezekiel's chariot or a gryphon. The sarcophagus to the west of the south door of the Baptistery in Florence has a gryphon on its east end.

7

The Crisis in the *Vita Nuova*

E. R. VINCENT

THE *Vita Nuova* is a book that has suffered at the hands of readers and expounders who have interpreted it according to their own particular tastes and beliefs. One only has to call to mind the visual images conjured up by the name of Dante Gabriel Rossetti, whose particular variety of nineteenth-century erotic romanticism had such an influence in this country; or of that of his father, old Gabriele Rossetti, who understood the book as a mystic conundrum and Beatrice herself as a symbol either of the Holy Roman Emperor, or of Dante's own soul.

A subtler understanding of the *Vita Nuova*, which can very easily lead to misunderstanding of the book, is that of those we may call the neo-Christian interpreters such as Charles Williams and his followers. They see Dante undergoing a mystic conversion into a 'Vita Nuova', a new life, similar to something they have, apparently, themselves experienced. Although some six hundred years intervene they use their own experience to explain Dante's. It is, of course, quite true that the *Vita Nuova* is the record of a fundamental change in its author. This change, however, was deeply personal to Dante and could not be defined or described by himself other than indirectly. Still less can others do so, however sincere they may be. When, for example, Charles Williams calls Beatrice 'the image of the redeemed life', or 'the way of the soul to its ordained end', he might be right, if he understood what Dante could not himself explain; on the other hand, one is inclined to suspect that he is quite wrong, for such expressions seem to reflect Charles Williams' own experience and not Dante's. He is certainly very far from Dante when he discusses from his personal standpoint, first and second loves, marriage and even divorce.[1]

Professor Charles S. Singleton in his work on the *Vita Nuova* is so far exalted by his own mysticism that he can write as follows: 'A reason why the complete seriousness of the *Vita Nuova* is beyond any question is that one of its authors—one of the authors of its prose—is God.'[2]

Those who stress the *conversion* aspect of the *Vita Nuova* like to understand the title of the book as meaning *New Life*. It is, however, generally accepted by Italian critics that it simply means *Youth*, as in *Purg.* xxx.115:

> Questi fu tal ne la sua vita nova,
> virtualmente, ch'ogni abito destro
> fatto averebbe in lui mirabil prova.

and we can compare the words 'l'età novella' used elsewhere, more than once, by Dante to mean a youthful age (*Inf.* xxxiii.88; *Par.* xvii.80). We can therefore deduce nothing from the title of the book as to any sort of conversion in Dante's life, religious or otherwise.

Let us repeat very simply what we know about the *Vita Nuova* from what Dante tells us and from the internal evidence of the book itself. It is a book about the period of his youth. From the chronology we are given by the author we can say that Dante and Beatrice first met as children in 1274; that the date of the first poem in the book is 1283; we can infer (but do not know) that the sonnet in para. ix

Cavalcando l'altr'ier per un cammino

was written in 1285; that para. xxii refers to the death of Beatrice's father (if Folco Portinari) in December 1289; that para. xxviii is to be dated 1290, the death of Beatrice; that para. xxxiv when Dante is discovered by visitors drawing an angel is 1291; that the Donna gentile (para. xxxv–xxxix) came on the scene after the second anniversary of Beatrice's death, i.e. after June 1292.

Neglecting the unproven supposition (Parodi) that there

---

[1] See Charles Williams, *The Figure of Beatrice: A Study in Dante* (Faber, 1953).
[2] *An Essay on the Vita Nuova* (Harvard U.P., 1949), p. 101.

were two different recensions of the *Vita Nuova*, of which only one has survived, we can say that the book consists of a prose commentary written (or at any rate finished) some time after 1292 to illustrate poems, the earliest of which is of 1283 and others of which can be dated 1285, 1289, and 1291. So far the humble but useful findings of chronology. Dante himself has divided the book into three main divisions according to subject: (1) Early poems up to § xix. (2) Poems chiefly concerned with the praise of Beatrice § xix to § xxx, *Materia di lode*. (3) § xxx to the end, sorrow for the death of Beatrice, a *nuova materia*. Neither the second nor the third division is solely concerned with the stated subjects: for example, the 'donna gentile' episode has almost the appearance of a postscript. Apart from these divisions the book is much influenced by caballistic numerology: the, to us, strange association of the number 9 with Beatrice is an example, and this influences the whole architecture where we find three equally spaced canzoni as the pillars of the edifice, flanked by a balanced order of shorter poems; so that we have 10 short poems, canzone i; 4 short poems, canzone ii, 4 short poems; canzone iii, 10 short poems. Within this careful framework we have all we know of Dante's youth and young manhood, and it is exactly what we should expect of a well-connected young Florentine in a time of great prosperity for the city. For the social background we have only to look into Villani's chronicle (vii.88) and see what was happening in the year of Dante's first sonnet:

In June 1283 for the feast of St. John, the city of Florence being in an excellent state and in great tranquillity, beneficial for merchants and manufacturers alike, especially for those of the Guelph party which ruled the city, there was organized in the Santa Felicità quarter beyond the Arno, a noble richly-dressed band of revellers all in white under the leadership of one who was called Love. These people were solely occupied in games and amusements, there was much dancing between gentlemen and ladies, 'popolani' and other excellent folk. They processed through the city blowing trumpets and playing other instruments. There were great banquets and supper parties and all rejoiced and it went on for nearly two months.

It was not really necessary for Dante to refer to the poets of antiquity to excuse his personification of love as a youth (para. xxv) when he and his readers had seen Love as a young man on horseback riding round the city and for two months presiding over a whole series of social functions. On the evidence of the *Vita Nuova* and viewed externally against his Florentine background we see Dante first as a young man of eighteen who has already taught himself to write poetry in the vulgar tongue and is sufficiently proficient to send a sonnet to the accepted poets of the day. We learn that he had thus found a great friend whom we know by the sonnet of reply to be Guido Cavalcanti; that he loves a girl called Bice or Beatrice; that he goes to church; that he takes part in an expedition, almost certainly military, in the direction of Arezzo; that he attends wedding-feasts and funerals, that he falls sick and suffers from an ocular complaint, that he is nursed by a sister, that he has friendly relations with a brother of Beatrice, that he can play music and draw pictures, but chiefly that he has a very extensive acquaintanceship with girls. Let us call them so, rather than *ladies* or *maidens*, which are words used to remove us one step farther from reality. For these charming creatures of the late thirteenth century, now so faint with the passing of the years and only alive by the grace of art, all those 'donne che hanno intelletto d'amore', those enigmatic 'screen-ladies', that sympathetic 'donna gentile', the gay group who mocked the love-sick young poet at the party, Beatrice herself, who is to end in splendid pre-eminence by the side of God in Paradise, were all just girls.

Poetry, music, art, social diversions, military adventure, friendship, and love is the tale of Dante's *Vita Nuova*, the days of his youth. We may think of him as that handsome sensitive young man of Giotto's fresco[1] in the Bargello, before the restorer ruined it, and forget the ascetic face based on a false tradition and spurious death-masks that has impressed its grim features on posterity.

Had Dante, however, been an ordinary gifted young man we should not have had anything more than a collection of not very distinguished poems in the Provençal convention, such as we find in the early part of the *Vita Nuova*. But something happened to him. It was not due to meeting

---

[1] The attribution of this fresco to Giotto is now doubted.

Beatrice either in childhood or youth; it was not due to the
death of Beatrice, for it occurred before that; it was not a
change from 'amor profano' to 'amor sacro' (Dante was no
less sensual after than before); it was not a change from
religious disbelief or indifference to formal belief (there is
no evidence that Dante was a better or worse 'credente' after
this crisis): but it was something so profound, absolute, and
lasting that it changed an imitative young poet into the man
who could write the *Divine Comedy*. It is no less than a
revolutionary change in his personality. He has told us
something about it, but it can be most clearly recognized
in the dramatic change in his poetry. The immediate
chronicle of the change begins in para. xvii and it is based
on dissatisfaction with himself and with his poetry. There
he speaks of the three preceding sonnets and says that along
those lines he had said all he could: 'però che mi parea di
me assai avere manifestato' and therefore he must change to
another nobler subject, 'matera nuova e più nobile che la
passata'. It is not, however, merely a change of poetical
subject or manner which is concerned, but a whole new
point of view. His relationship with the second screen-lady,
whatever it may have been, gave cause for scandal (para. x):
'troppa gente ne ragionava oltre li termini de la cortesia'
and Beatrice cuts him in the street, 'passando per alcuna
parte, mi negò lo suo dolcissimo salutare'. Dante is enormously distressed. He is still more so when at a large gathering
for a marriage feast he is so much overcome by the sight of
Beatrice that he lays himself open to mockery. A bevy of
girls, with Beatrice amongst them, smile and whisper as the
love-struck youth seeks support at the wall. It is one of
those scenes as in a Giotto fresco that strike the imagination
of the reader. In the privacy of his own room he considers
the whole situation and the course of his love or loves, of his
attitude to Beatrice and to other women. Finally, he falls
asleep 'come un pargoletto battuto lagrimando', like a
beaten child. Love appears to him in a dream-vision and
tells him to give over these secondary attachments (simul-
acra nostra) and further proclaims in Latin, the hierarchical
tongue: 'Ego tanquam centrum circuli, cui simili modo se
habent circumferentie partes; tu autem non sic.'

Real love is balanced, in poise, spins even, includes the rest of life and is included in it, but Dante is off-centre, eccentric, distraught, and wrong. The three previous sonnets he mentioned in para. xvii, well illustrate his condition:

> Tutti li miei penser parlan d'Amore;
> e hanno in lor sì gran varietate,
> ch'altro mi fa voler sua potestate,
> altro folle ragiona il suo valore,
> altro sperando m'apporta dolzore,
> altro pianger mi fa spesse fiate;
> e sol s'accordano in cherer pietate,
> tremando di paura che è nel core.   (xiii)

His troubled state of anguish produces some very bad verses:

> Ciò che m'incontra, ne la mente more,
> quand' i' vegno a veder voi, bella gioia;
> e quand' io vi son presso, i' sento Amore
> che dice: 'Fuggi, se 'l perir t'è noia'.
> Lo viso mostra lo color del core,
> che, tramortendo, ovunque pò s'appoia;
> e per la ebrietà del gran tremore
> le pietre par che gridin: Moia, moia.   (xv)

Love assails him as an enemy, and he suffers pain and is threatened with actual death. This is the Dante before the crisis. Now in the enormously important paragraphs xviii and xix we have the resolution of the crisis and the blossoming forth of the new Dante. Suitably enough it is in the company of girls that he sees the way he should go. It is feminine sympathy he needs, but of course only of those women 'che sono gentili e che non sono pure femmine'. It is only with those 'Donne ch' hanno intelletto d'amore' he can discuss and resolve the intimate secrets of his heart. It is a smiling, half-flirtatious discussion, in which the bald kernel is this: 'Whatever, my dear Dante, is the sense of your love for Beatrice, seeing that you swoon when you see her?' 'My only joy,' he replies, 'is in writing poems of praise of her.' 'Why don't you do so, then?' they respond with a feminine sense of the actual and no doubt thinking of his three recent sonnets. He leaves them ashamed, for he knows

that his poetry has so far been unworthy: 'E però propuosi
di prendere per matera de lo mio parlare sempre mai quello
che fosse loda di questa gentilissima; e pensando molto a
ciò, pareami avere impresa troppo alta matera quanto a me,
sì che non ardia di cominciare; e così dimorai alquanti dì
con disiderio di dire e con paura di cominciare.' What he
had in mind was no formal change of subject or style. He
was overcome with a new resolution, he was filled with a
sense of a new creation and he was afraid to limit his burning
thoughts within the actual bounds of verse. He waited some
days, longing to write and fearing to do so 'con disiderio di
dire e con paura di cominciare'. What does a poet do in
such a period of gestation? He goes for a walk by himself in
the country, and being a Florentine he passes beyond the
walls and goes through the meadows skirting the Arno.

Avvenne poi che passando per uno cammino lungo lo quale sen gia
uno rivo chiaro molto, a me giunse tanta volontade di dire, che io
cominciai a pensare lo modo ch'io tenesse; e pensai che parlare di lei
non si convenia che io facesse, se io non parlasse a donne in seconda
persona, e non ad ogni donna, ma solamente a coloro che sono gentili
e che non sono pure femmine. Allora dico che la mia lingua parlò
quasi come per se stessa mossa, e disse: *Donne ch'avete intelletto
d'amore*. Queste parole io ripuosi ne la mente con grande letizia,
pensando di prenderle per mio cominciamento; onde poi, ritornato a
la sopradetta cittade, pensando alquanti die, cominciai una canzone
con questo cominciamento, ordinata nel modo che si vedrà di sotto
ne la sua divisione. La canzone comincia: *Donne ch'avete*.

Here we have a great poet describing in detail the steps
of his evolving inspiration. First dissatisfaction, then the
idea of a basic theme, then the days of half-unconscious
rumination, then the moment when with the sudden
appearance of a perfect opening line '*Donne ch'avete intelletto d'amore* the full flood of inspiration is released, and after
some days of technical elaboration the first great poem of
Dante's production is committed to paper.

Dante himself had no doubts about the novelty and
importance of this poem: 'io t'ho allevata per figliuola
d'Amor giovane e piana', he says in the concluding stanza.
When he pretends to meet a brother poet, Bonagiunta of

Lucca, in Purgatory (*Purg.* xxiv.49) he is greeted with delight as follows:

> Ma dì s' i' veggio qui colui che fore
> trasse le nove rime, cominciando
> *'Donne ch'avete intelletto d'amore'.*

Are you really the author of that wonderfully original poem? And Dante replies with the well-known lines that he is one who only writes when love inspires him.

> 'I' mi son un, che quando
> Amor mi spira, noto, e a quel modo
> ch' e' ditta dentro vo significando'.

In the great poem, *Al cor gentil repara sempre Amore,* Guido Guinizelli had formulated the philosophy of love which was to guide Dante from this point onwards. The older poet had already promoted his lady to heaven, and Dante is not original in his angelization of Beatrice. Dante, however, is a supreme poet and in sonnets written in the new mood such as:

> Tanto gentile e tanto onesta pare
> la donna mia quand'ella altrui saluta

> Vede perfettamente onne salute
> chi la mia donna tra le donne vede

in such poems as these we have the highest expression of Tuscan poetry.

That Dante was consciously following Guinizelli we can see in the sonnet that immediately follows the canzone *Donne ch'avete* (para. xx);

> Amore e 'l cor gentil sono una cosa,
> sì come il saggio in suo dittare pone.

Love and a 'cor gentil' *are* the same thing, as the sage poet Guinizelli said in his well-known poem:

> e così esser l'un sanza l'altro osa
> come alma razional sanza razione,

and one can no more exist apart from the other than a reasonable mind without reason. Guinizelli's theory of love, stated in the simplest possible terms, was that it is an innate faculty of certain sensitive persons and such are distinguished by their intrinsic merit; the faculty of love cannot be inherited, for it is not a nobility such as the world understands the term.

The next outstanding formulation of a love theory in poetry was by Dante's friend Guido Cavalcanti in his extremely difficult philosophical poem, *Donna me prega*. Here it is stated that, far from being innate in the chosen few, it is an external force from without that strikes its victim like a thunderbolt and with equally distressing effects. Its place is not the heart but the mind where it unseats reason and leads to all those unreasonable actions associated with the behaviour of lovers. It drives them distracted. Despite the anguish and even death which it can cause, love is a good thing. It is a most contradictory understanding of the phenomenon of love. Now a glance at the early poems of the *Vita Nuova* is enough to show that the young Dante is in accord with his friend Cavalcanti in his understanding of love. The poems record a sorrowful battle

> s'elli è dolore alcun, quanto 'l mio, grave;
> . . . . . .
> s'io son d'ogni tormento ostale e chiave.   (vii)
>
> le pietre par che gridin: Moia, moia.   (xv)
>
> ch'Amor m'assale subitamente
> sì che la vita quasi m'abbandona.   (xvi)

It is not, I think, too fanciful to suppose that after the first two verses of the sonnet in § xx which hail Guinizelli as a love philosopher, the following two verses:

> e così esser l'un sanza l'altro osa
> com' alma razional sanza ragione,

are a conscious refutation of Cavalcanti, for the latter expressly states that love drives out reason from a rational mind. Be that as it may, one aspect of the change in Dante is that Guinizelli's influence prevails over that of Cavalcanti and the real poet Dante is born. The death of Beatrice is a central point in the book, but it is not described nor are its immediate effects. The poet that was born with the canzone *Donne ch'avete intelletto d'amore* had already achieved such a stature that he could survive this blow and absorb its effects into his art and life and eventually give us the *Divine Comedy*. We cannot, it is foolish to try, define the meaning of the fundamental change mirrored in paragraphs xviii–xix of the *Vita Nuova*, though we can recognize its effects. Dante's life is suddenly concentric, love and life are one, and to use his own image the wheel is balanced, an image which he repeats at the topmost height of Paradise:

> Ma già volgeva il mio disio e il velle,
> sì come rota ch' igualmente è mossa,
> l'amor che move il sole e l'altre stelle.

Dante could not, of course, maintain this supreme sureness that first came to him as he, a troubled young man, walked along the Arno and sought for inspiration. The 'Donna gentile' episode is obviously a renewal of stress and strain, however Dante allegorizes it later. And at some time between the final pages of the *Vita Nuova* and his exile comes the so-called period of aberration when in the company of Forese Donati and others he led a far from balanced life. The wheel often swung away off-centre. There was a time when the 'diritta via' was 'smarrita' and he found himself in such a dark and tangled wood that he nearly perished:

> 'Tant'è amara che poco è più morte'

But he never forgot that first tremendous vision of truth and its personification in the young girl Beatrice:

> Alcun tempo il sostenni col mio volto:
> mostrando li occhi giovanetti a lui,
> meco il menava in dritta parte volto.   (*Purg.* xxx. 115)

But not for long, because he was deflected:

> e volse i passi suoi per via non vera,
> imagini di ben seguendo false,
> che nulla promission rendono intera.   (Ibid. 130)

It is most significant that late in his life, when he was writing the concluding cantos of the *Purgatorio*, he harks back to the period of his first experience of revelation when Beatrice was alive. It is his admission that the moment of truth that came to him in the Florentine countryside and which he has described in paragraphs xvii, xviii, and xix of the *Vita Nuova* was the turning-point of his life. That such a high plane of all-embracing understanding could not always be maintained was natural and inevitable, but it was never forgotten and it was the first spark that kindled the great glow of inspiration that gave the world the *Divina Commedia*. Let us not therefore underrate its importance and let us not succumb to the temptation of attempting to explain it in the terms of our own experience. The revelations of love are personal and they are private.

Appendix

The Oxford Dante Society

THE Oxford Dante Society owes its origin to the Rev.
Edward Moore, Principal of St. Edmund Hall, in
conjunction with Signor de Tivoli (Taylorian lecturer
in Italian), the Rev. H. F. Tozer (Exeter), the Rev. G. W.
Kitchin (Christ Church) and the Rev. E. G. Livingstone
(Pembroke), and its first meeting was held in St. Edmund
Hall on 24 November 1876. The Society was to meet once
a term (and the day came to be fixed to the fifth Tuesday of
each term), being entertained to dinner ('of an ordinary
description') by the members in turn. The objects of the
Society were defined as 'to read papers and discuss subjects
connected with Dante: to encourage mutual inquiry as to
critical, historical and other points relating to his works:
to interchange information as to new books, reviews,
monographs, etc., and generally to stimulate and forward
the study of the *Divina Commedia*, and other works of
Dante and of his age.' A paper was to be read at each meeting
by a member 'as far as possible in rotation in order of
seniority'. The Society consisted at the outset of ten members, but the number was later increased to twelve and for a
time to fifteen. There are also Honorary Members, not
included in the quota. Meetings have been held regularly
without interruption, except in November 1914, and in
November 1939, May 1941, and February 1942. The
Society has no officers except an honorary secretary, of
which there have been four, Edward Moore, Paget Toynbee,
W. H. V. Reade, and C. G. Hardie.

In 1920 the then Secretary, Paget Toynbee, compiled
and had privately printed in 102 copies a detailed record of
the Society in its first forty-four years (to 1920) 'in view of
the approaching celebration of the sixth centenary of the
death of Dante'. The following supplementary list of
members up to 1963 is compiled in view of the seventh

centenary in 1965 of Dante's birth. The first thirty-nine names are taken from Paget Toynbee's list, with the addition of the dates of death subsequent to 1920.

LIST OF MEMBERS

1. (Elected 24 November 1876) *Rev. Edward Moore, Principal of St. Edmund Hall. (†2 September 1916.)
2. (24 November 1876) *Rev. George William Kitchin, Christ Church. (*R.* 3 November 1883; † 14 October 1912.)
3. (24 November 1876) *Rev. Henry Fanshawe Tozer, Exeter. (*R.* 9 December 1900; †2 June 1916.)
4. (24 November 1876) *Rev. Robert George Livingstone, Pembroke. (*R.* 21 November 1896; †23 June 1935.)
5. (24 November 1876) *Rev. Thomas Kelly Cheyne, Balliol. (*R.* 16 October 1889; † 16 February 1915.)
6. (24 November 1876) *Rev. William Walrond Jackson, Exeter. (†29 August 1931.)
7. (24 November 1876) *Rev. Archibald Henry Sayce, Queen's. (*R.* 23 October 1890; †4 February 1933.)
8. (24 November 1876) *Vitale De Tivoli. (†17 June 1883.)
9. (24 November 1876) *Robert Laing (afterwards Cuthbert Shields), C.C.C. (*R.* 25 May 1880; †20 September 1908.)
10. (24 November 1876) *Rev. John Earle, Oriel. (*R.* 23 February 1895; †31 January 1903.)
11. (6 March 1877) Charles Lancelot Shadwell, Oriel. (*R.* 11 November 1913; †13 February 1919.)
12. (4 December 1878) Rev. Henry Parry Liddon, D.D., Christ Church. (†9 September 1890.)
13. (5 February 1881) Rev. William Wolfe Capes, Hertford. (*R.* 27 May 1885; †31 October 1914.)
14. (7 June 1881) Frederick York Powell, Christ Church. (†8 May 1904.)

* Original Member.   † Died.   R. Resigned.

15. (3 November 1883) James Bryce, Oriel. (*R.* 3 June 1902; †22 January 1922.)
16. (3 November 1883) Edward Armstrong, Queen's. (†14 April 1928.)
17. (27 May 1885) Rev. Charles William Boase, Exeter. (*R.* 22 November 1893; †11 March 1895.)
18. (7 November 1890) Rev. Francis Paget, D.D., Christ Church (*R.* 19 November 1903; †2 August 1911.)
19. (7 November 1890) Rev. Charles Plummer, C.C.C. (*R.* 19 November 1903; †8 September 1927.)
20. (1 December 1890) Walter Horatio Pater, Brasenose. (†30 July 1894.)
21. (1 December 1890) Thomas Herbert Warren, President of Magdalen. (*R.* 3 June 1924; †9 June 1930.)
22. (6 February 1894) William Paton Ker, All Souls. (†17 July 1923.)
23. (23 February 1895) Paul Ferdinand Willert, Exeter. (*R.* 21 February 1911; †4 March 1912.)
24. (15 June 1895) Paget Jackson Toynbee, Balliol. (†13 May 1932.)
25. (15 June, 1895) John Alexander Stewart, Christ Church. (*R.* 11 November 1930; †27 December 1933.)
26. (4 March 1897) Edward Caird, Master of Balliol. (*R.* 12 November 1907; †1 November 1908.)
27. (5 June 1900) Rev. Sir John Caesar Hawkins, Bart., Oriel. (*R.* 12 November 1901; †18 January 1920.)
28. (3 June 1902) Very Rev. Thomas Banks Strong, D.D., Dean of Christ Church. (*R.* 9 November 1937; †8 June 1944.)
29. (3 June 1902) Bernard William Henderson, Exeter. (*R.* 24 February 1904; †11 January 1929.)
30. (24 February 1904) David Binning Monro, Provost of Oriel. (†22 August 1905.)
31. (24 February 1904) Percy Ewing Matheson, New College. (*R.* 18 February 1936; †11 May 1946.)
32. (15 November 1904) Rev. William Holden Hutton, St. John's. (*R.* 27 May 1930; †24 October 1930.)

† Died.　　　　　　　*R.* Resigned.

33. (15 November 1904) Louis Dyer, Balliol. (†20 July 1908.)

34. (6 March 1905) Charles Buller Heberden, Principal of Brasenose. († 30 May 1921.)

35. (19 May 1908) John William Mackail, Balliol. (*R.* 22 February 1927; †13 December 1945.)

36. (10 November 1908) William Henry Vincent Reade, Keble. († December 1944.)

37. (14 November 1911) (Professor) Cesare Foligno, Queen's. (†9 November 1963.)

38. (9 February 1915) Geoffrey Baskerville, Keble. (*R.* 30 May 1916. †   ?   .)

39. (29 May 1917) Rev. Frank Edward Brightman, Magdalen. († 31 March 1932.)

40. (15 November 1921) Dr. Francis William Pember, Warden of All Souls. (*R.* 16 February 1937; †19 January 1954.)

41. (19 February 1924) Rev. Herbert Edward Douglas Blakiston, President of Trinity. (*R.* 8 November 1938; †30 September 1942.)

42. (11 November 1924) (Professor) Ernest Fraser Jacob, All Souls.

43. (15 November 1927) Professor George Albert Cooke, Christ Church. (*R.* 18 February 1936; †3 September 1939.)

44. (15 November 1927) John Edward Austin Joliffe, Keble. (*R.* 25 May 1954; †13 January 1964.)

45. (12 February 1929) Benedict Humphrey Sumner, Balliol, later Warden of All Souls. (*R.* 14 November 1944; re-elected 29 May 1945; *R.* 8 November 1950; †25 April 1951.)

46. (4 June 1929) Professor Clement Charles Julian Webb, Oriel, later Magdalen. (*R.* 11 November 1952; †5 October 1954.)

47. (11 November 1930) Professor Richard MacGillivray Dawkins, Exeter. († 4 May 1955.)

48. (26 May 1931) (Professor) Eric Reginald Pearce Vincent, Christ Church. (*R.* 14 February 1939.)

† Died.   *R.* Resigned.

49. (24 May 1932) Professor (Sir) Maurice Powicke, Oriel. (*R.* 8 November 1950; †19 May 1963.)
50. (2 June 1936) Professor Alfred Ewert, Trinity.
51. (10 November 1936) Professor William James Entwistle, Exeter. († 13 June 1952.)
52. (16 February 1937) (Professor) Clive Staples Lewis, Magdalen. (*R.* 28 May 1957; †22 November 1963.)
53. (24 May 1938) Colin Graham Hardie, Magdalen.
54. (24 May 1939) Professor (Sir) Cyril N. Hinshelwood, Exeter.
55. (24 May 1939) Rev. Fr. Martin Cyril D'Arcy, S.J., Master of Campion Hall. (*R.* 13 November 1945.)
56. (15 February 1944) (Sir) Cecil Maurice Bowra, Warden of Wadham. (*R.* 27 May 1952.)
57. (15 February 1944) Charles Walter Stansby Williams. (†15 May 1945.)
58. (20 February 1945) Professor John Ronald Reuel Tolkien, Pembroke, later Merton. (*R.* 15 February 1955.)
59. (28 May 1946) Professor Alexander Passerin d'Entrèves, Magdalen. (*R.* 12 November 1957.)
60. (27 May 1952) (Professor) Richard William Southern, Balliol and All Souls.
61. (11 November 1952) Dr. Lorenzo Minio-Paluello, Oriel.
62. (26 May 1953) Professor Jean Seznec, All Souls.
63. (9 November 1954) Charles Alan Robson, Christ Church.
64. (8 November 1955) (Professor) Cecil Grayson, St. Edmund Hall, later Magdalen.
65. (14 February 1956) Professor Peter Edward Lionel Russell, Russell, Exeter.
66. (18 February 1958) John Rigby Hale, Jesus College.
67. (18 February 1958) Professor Edgar Wind, Trinity.
68. (23 February 1960) Professor Thomas Bertram Wallace Reid, Trinity.

† Died.   *R.* Resigned.